LIFE IS DOPE

15 STORIES OF HARD-WON HOPE & THE POWER OF PERSEVERANCE

MICHAEL ANTHONY

Copyright © 2025 by Big Plan Holdings LLC

All rights reserved. This book or any portion thereof may not be reproduced or used in any manner whatsoever without the express written permission of the publisher except for the use of brief quotations in a book review.

This book does not contain medical, psychological, financial or health advice. It provides information for general and educational purposes only.

This nonfiction book contains true stories from the author's life. Extremely minor adjustments have been made in a few rare spots for communication purposes. Several names were changed for privacy reasons. There are no major events, lessons and major aspects of this book that are fiction.

Published in the United States of America

www.michaelanthonytv.com

TABLE OF CONTENTS

Dedication 7

Introduction 9
Life Can Be Dope 9
    Where to Begin 10
    Fragments 11

A Note About Music 13

Story 1: The Bad News Is the Good News 15
    What Was That? 15
    A Fitting End? 16
    Trying on Adulthood 18
    Fleeing for My Life 21
    Making Sense of the Senseless 22
    Transforming Setbacks into Significance 25
    Making Life Dope: 25

Story 2: Act Like an Owner 27
    The Freedom of the Cage 28
    Digging Through Rubble 29
    Owning My Destiny 31
    Loving What Is 32
    The Gift of Adversity 34
    Claiming Ownership of Your Journey 37
    Making Life Dope: 38

Story 3: You're Meant for More 41
    Flavor of Inspiration 43
    Hope Against Hope 46

    Standing on the Brink. 48
    Making Life Dope:. 50

Story 4: Success Comes to Those Who Persevere 53
    A Message in the Storm 55
    A Decent Meal. 57
    The Challenge and Reward of Perseverance 58
    Making Life Dope:. 59

Story 5: Flip the Coin. 61
    A Wake-Up Call. 63
    Flip the Coin 64
    A Dead End 66
    The Other Side of the Coin 67
    Getting Real 70
    Delivering Value 71
    The Flip Side of Challenge 73
    Making Life Dope:. 74

Story 6: Fill Your Space 77
    From the Sales Floor to the Sales Lot 79
    Feeling the Heat. 80
    Looking Again to Escape 82
    A Lesson From the Past 83
    Embracing Growth Through Tension 84
    Making Life Dope:. 86

Story 7: Know The Game You're Playing 89
    The Game of (Your) Life. 91
    Run Your Race 93
    Success on Your Terms 95
    Creating Your Own Scorecard. 96
    Making Life Dope:. 96

Story 8: People Like Us Do Things Like This 99
    Among the Minions 102
    Taking the Stage 104
    Uncovering Who You've Always Been 105
    Making Life Dope:. 108

Story 9: The Future Is a Fairy Tale 111
    A Selfie to Remember. 114
    Getting Your Money's Worth. 115
    Memories That Last 117
    Making Life Dope:. 119

Story 10: Four-Letter Words. 121
    There is No Try 122
    Stop Should-ing on Yourself 125
    The Most Sinister Four-Letter Word of All 128
    Fuck Around and Find Out 131
    Making Life Dope:. 132

Story 11: Design a Life You Don't Need a Vacation From 135
    A Chance Meeting. 136
    No Vacation Required. 138
    What's Next?. 139
    Be Here on the Way There 141
    Content And Never Satisfied. 142
    Making Life Dope:. 144

Story 12: Your #1 Investment 147
    Investing in Yourself. 148
    Misguided Priorities 150
    Me Inc. 151
    The Best Bet. 152
    Putting Your Money Where Your Mouth Is. 154
    Making Life Dope:. 156

Story 13: The Greatest Gifts Are Those You Give 159
   Turning Forty. 160
   Cultivating Generosity 162
   40K for 40. 163
   Open Hands, Full Soul 166
   Making Life Dope:. 168

Story 14: Opportunities Come With an Expiration Date 171
   Wrecked 173
   A Legacy at Stake. 175
   Living Into Your Legacy 177
   Making Life Dope:. 178

Story 15: I'm Not Broken, I'm a Prism. 181
   Broken. 182
   Emergency Intervention. 183
   Perfectly Imperfect 186
   Own Your Weird 188
   My Life is Dope 190
   Making Life Dope:. 191

Conclusion: What's Next. 193
   You. 195
   The Present and the Possible 196
   Inflection Point 197
   Remember This 198

Acknowledgments 201

Endnotes 202

DEDICATION

Sarah, thank you for all the years of growing up together. Even now, that we're apart, I am still your #1 fan and want nothing but the best for you!

Mikayla, you made me a father and gave me a reason to grow into who I am today. I love you more than you'll ever know. Keep changing the world!

Matthew, you are my heart. It's an honor to call you my son. I love you so freaking much!

Without the three of you, I wouldn't be who I am and this book wouldn't exist. I thank God for gifting me with you in my life!

xoxo

INTRODUCTION

Life Can Be Dope

What you hold in your hands isn't just a book. It's a collection of raw, unfiltered glimpses into my life. My intention is to lay myself bare, showing you the humiliation of my mistakes and the humility earned through those experiences. These are the stories behind my deepest scars and the wisdom I drew from each.

Ultimately, though, this is a book about hope—not some wish-upon-a-star type of hope. This isn't about standing on the shoreline waiting for God to part the seas so you can waltz across to your dreams.

No, this is the kind of hope that's hard-won. It's sprouted from nothing and cultivated every day. And it's *real* hope, the kind that can be relied on. Because it grew on the belief that, no matter what happens, you will choose the best response to whatever comes your way. Ultimately, the hope you'll learn about in these pages is rooted in ownership.

This is also a guide to rediscovery. I'll take you on a journey that proves a great life isn't found in perfection but in embracing brokenness. Every obstacle you encounter can lead you to your truest self. Sometimes who we are gets buried under the burdens and baggage we accumulate over the course of a lifetime. But we are all called to find the gift of authenticity within ourselves.

As you read, you'll see how the unique aspects of our personalities, whether born from trauma or inherent traits, refract life's light in ways no "normal" lens could. This book will explore how our imperfections can become sources of grace and healing, not just for ourselves but for those around us. By the end, you'll understand that true freedom and fulfillment come not from erasing our broken parts, but from celebrating them for the complexity and depth they add to our existence. Like a prism channeling universal light, we each have the potential to impact the world profoundly and positively.

The journey through life isn't about becoming someone new. We rediscover the essence of who we have always been by pushing against our limits and leaning into faith on the path toward a vision of what could be.

You might feel as though you've lost touch with yourself—that part of you that's uniquely powerful. In the pages ahead, you'll see that I can relate. I remember a time when I seriously doubted if I had a "higher self" to connect with. But somewhere deep inside, I could hear its whisper and sense its presence.

This book is for you if you're in that place of doubt, searching for a path that will bring you back to your inner strength. I believe this force guides each of us, if we allow it, toward understanding that we were born for more. That we're capable of achieving beyond what our current, limited imaginations can conceive.

When we allow ourselves to be laid bare, only *then* can our true self—the imprint of the Divine, the incredible power that has been with us since before our existence began—reveal itself. It's a journey of discovery and rediscovery, leading to a connection with the essence of who we are.

> It's a journey of discovery and rediscovery.

Let's take it together.

Where to Begin

Most books are read by less than half of the people who buy them. So while I hope this is helpful enough for you to finish, I understand some people won't. That's why, instead of writing one big book, I assembled a series of short stories, each communicating a principle I learned through living it. Remember those scars I mentioned?

Yes, many lessons build on the others, so it's best you read in order. But if you prefer to skip around, then go right ahead—each chapter is designed to stand on its own.

This is my story. It wasn't always sunshine and rainbows. Far from it. But I'm still standing. And as I've lived out these experiences, what's driven me is the hope to eventually be on the "other side" and empower others with the principles that drove me to persevere.

Today, I stand before you stronger, wiser, and healthier than ever. Yes, I'm still a work-in-progress (read: hot mess) in many areas of my life, and I'm also overflowing with love and gratitude. I've come to realize that my many challenges happened *for* me, not *to* me. As the rapper T.I. says, "Pain is a small thing to a giant." I've embraced my hardships, and they've made me who I am today.

Those closest to me know I'm always intentional with my words. Having said that, I'd like to share a couple of caveats.

Fragments

First, there are *many* examples in this book where I share some unkind opinions and less-than-flattering sides of myself and others. I've wrestled with including it all, even to the point of not writing this book, for fear of painting anyone in a negative light. The hesitation stems from a trend in today's world, where we so often throw stones from a distance.

So, let me say for the record that *every one* of the individuals who appear in my story had and have beautiful and loving sides alongside the darker ones, as we all do. I highly respect, love, and cherish most, if not all, of them.

And I can say with utmost sincerity that I'm grateful for the role each played in my story. I'm thankful for my Creator, family, former bosses, pastors, and friends. And I deeply love and respect my parents.

My second caveat is this: comparison is a punk. If you find yourself comparing your experience to mine, you're missing the point.

I wouldn't change a single thing about my journey, and I wouldn't wish it on anyone. At the same time, I understand there are millions, possibly even you reading this right now, who have lives that make mine look like a walk in the park.

Nothing I've included here is intended for my glory, my ego, or your sympathy. I share all of this, especially the intimate and unfiltered, with the sole purpose of you finding a part of your own story in these pages. This is my love letter to hope, who was my constant companion through every story you're about to read.

I want you to lean into your hope, founded on the faith that you're worth fighting for. I want you to realize the power you possess not just to carry on, but to conquer. I want you to discover your ability to leave behind a life of indecision, ambiguity, and pain, and step into a life of strength. A life lived to its fullest and on your own terms.

> There is hope.

If I ended up here, persevering through all the stories you're about to hear, then I hope you'll agree: there is hope.

I invite you to engage with me and "play full out" in reading this book from cover to cover. I encourage you to interact with the material along the way. Listen to the music, take notes, journal, reflect, and dive deeper into *your* journey through the exercises offered throughout. If you accept my invitation, I know a brighter "future you" will greet you on the other end.

A NOTE ABOUT MUSIC

Music has been a constant in my life. Without it, I wouldn't be who or where I am today. It's not an understatement to say that I may not be alive without music. At the beginning of each chapter, you'll find the lyrics to a song that convey the spirit of the message, along with a QR Code to a Spotify playlist.

I've set it up this way with the intention of you listening to these songs *before* reading each story to let the energy, the meaning of the words, and the emotion of the songs wash over you and penetrate your soul as they have mine. I've played these songs hundreds of times. No exaggeration. They've kept me grounded, guided me through some of my darkest hours, and helped to cultivate the optimistic and confident outlook on life I have. Scan the QR code below and follow my Spotify profile to keep these (and other) playlists at your fingertips.

These songs have been my lifelines, and my heart's prayer is that they will resonate with you in the same way they have with me. So get comfortable, cue up the LID Book playlist, and let's dive in!

Follow Michael Anthony's Spotify Playlists

Listen to the LID Book Playlist

STORY 1

The Bad News Is the Good News

*It's beyond my control sometimes it's best to let go,
whatever happens in this lifetime
So I trust in love (So I trust in love)
You have given me peace of mind*
—POD, "Alive"

What Was That?

It was 1997, the era when bass was king in hip hop, when the "808" and "909" kicks from your Alpine stereo announced your arrival from the next county over. So as my friends Joe, Marcus, and Tyrell jumped into the rear passenger door of my '87 Olds Cutlass Ciera, their greetings muffled by the new Boogiemonsters album booming from the stereo, I wasn't sure if the faint pops I'd heard were gunshots.

A quick glance at my side and rear view mirrors cleared my mind—I didn't see anything or anyone unusual. Of course, it was dark, like the hood is at 11:30 p.m. on a Saturday. And maybe I did hear gunshots, like you do in the hood at 11:30 p.m. on a Saturday. But this was home sweet home, and I wasn't concerned.

That night was my first time at Tyrell's house. He lived by the railroad tracks in Phillips, a neighborhood on the southside of Minneapolis a few blocks from where I lived. Marcus was a close friend; Tyrell was more of an acquaintance, but I hadn't seen him in months and was glad when Marcus asked if he could bring him along.

As Marcus pushed his way in to make room for Tyrell, his leg got stuck between the seat and the massive, two-sided cassette case in the floorboard. Seeing this, I started laughing as I helped dislodge his leg and make room for Tyrell.

That's when I heard another pop. But this time, there was no doubt—that was a gunshot, and it was *close*.

Eyes wide, I looked over the back seat, and I saw an image that remains burned into my brain decades later—three figures no more than ten feet away, framed in the October air's soft mist and silhouetted by the street lights at their back. Then, a burst of orange blew out the glass of my rear window.

> "Get down! They're shooting!"

Slamming the pedal to the floor, I yelled to my friends: "Get down! They're shooting!"

A Fitting End?

Not even two months after my eighteenth birthday, I'd already been through so much for so long that I was effectively numb. A bullet to the head would've fit the narrative. *"What's next? Oh, this? Okay, why not!?"*

So what had happened up to this point? Let's review:

- Born August of 1979 just outside of New York City in Bronxville, NY to a teen mother who struggled with drug

addiction and dabbled in prostitution before abandoning me at age one to become a high-end escort in Texas.
- Sexual abuse started earlier than I can remember, and memories that began at three years old when my grandfather, the same man who sexually abused my mother, turned his perversion toward me and warned me to keep it "our little secret."
- Abducted from preschool by my grandpa, who snatched me up without telling my grandmother. He moved me to Minnesota to meet my mother at four years old after completing nine months of rehab.
- Sexual abuse resumed almost immediately, starting with a new babysitter who promised to "show me everything" if I'd touch her as instructed, and continuing onto multiple other babysitters.
- Repeatedly sexually assaulted by the boyfriend of my best friend's mom.
- Left alone in a filthy home from age five. The same year I became responsible for cleaning *everything*, all the way down to the poop and pee of the dogs' mom left me to care for.
- At age eight, my babysitter, the daughter of a family friend, called me into her room to show me that she was organizing ten piles of ten pills, explaining that she planned to take a pile every eight minutes until she was dead. Thankfully, her parents' arrival thwarted her finality.
- Waiting around until midnight for my mom and step-father—the man who lovingly adopted me and I proudly call "Dad"—to return home from their ministry work. At times, I resorted to mac and Coca-Cola for sustenance—not mac and cheese washed down with a nice Coca-Cola; mac and cheese *made* with the open cokes my mom didn't finish because there was no milk or butter, and water was too bland.

- Physical and verbal abuse from Dad, being thrown across the room into walls, hearing him call the dogshit laying around the house "little Mikes."
- A move from the suburbs to downtown Minneapolis, where I would repeatedly be threatened and stabbed in the neck and head for the color of my skin, and where I now found myself a sitting duck to the people gunning me down.

As you can see, I'd been taking an ass-kicking since birth. If ever anyone could claim the role of victim, it was me, so why not add "shooting victim" to the list? I was used to this. Over time, I had learned to cope with it all through a simple, calloused attitude toward a life where I'd learned the best I could hope for was survival: *it is what it is. Make the best of it.* And this was what it was, the potential knockout blow that would finally put an end to a relentless eighteen-year-long beating.

> I'd been taking an ass-kicking since birth.

Trying on Adulthood

In the months leading up to the shooting, I had a much clearer idea of what I didn't want than what I did. Having just graduated high school, I knew I didn't want to borrow twenty grand to take classes I didn't care about. I didn't want to *maybe* figure out what I wanted to do with my life, and then *maybe* dig myself out of debt. And I knew there was a good chance I could figure out my future and end up in a better financial position by just taking a minimum wage job. Enter Marshalls, Mall of America, shoe department.

> I knew I didn't want to borrow twenty grand to take classes I didn't care about.

Despite the shitty pay, the job marked my first adult decision and what I hoped would be the end of the continuous string of bad hands I'd been dealt in life. Nevertheless, the best part of the job was clocking out. So when we closed at 9:30 p.m. on that fateful night and I'd washed the foot residue from my hands, I hurried out to what had become a Saturday tradition. I jumped into my car, made a beeline to the Taco Bell drive-thru for some fifty-nine cent tacos, then proceeded down Highway 77, past the wealthy side of Minneapolis, and into the not-rich inner city to pick up my friends. We were headed to a new ministry intended for people who otherwise wouldn't step foot in a traditional church.

Rewind to a few weeks earlier— as I was leaving my house to head to the mall, I'd spotted a postcard advertising a new midnight church service. It was hosted every Saturday by a Christian music venue. By this point, I had abandoned church after seventeen years of regular attendance. My decision to leave organized religion was no accident—far from it. There were a number of factors that led me to jump ship, but they boiled down to a growing disgust with churches doling out and tolerating an endless stream of bullshit in the name of the God I loved.

My mom took the brunt of what I witnessed. Despite cleaning up her act and becoming an ordained minister—a damn good one, I might add—she had to walk through miles of the church's bullshit on the path to becoming Minneapolis' first female police chaplain.

She had two strikes against her. The first was her gender. I probably don't have to tell you that many churches justify a lot of chauvinism and small-dick energy based on their interpretations of bible verses about "male authority" and "female submission." In the process, they overlook that the same book they use to treat women as inferiors makes plain that we're *all* made in God's image, not just the ones with penises.

But back to what I was saying—I watched as church after church and denomination after denomination leeched off of her time and energy while denying her the title of "Children's Pastor." Instead, they granted her its unofficial, unpaid alternative: *Children's Minister*. This would go on until, eventually, a male came along to claim the title of "Pastor," undoing her progress and collecting the paychecks owed to her tireless and "faithful" efforts.

The second strike against her was her divorce. Nevermind that she got married at eighteen and divorced around eighteen and a half. Nevermind that she had cleaned herself up, remarried as an older adult, and was fully committed to her new husband, the man I proudly called "Dad." And nevermind that some of the pastors judging her to be morally unfit to serve in an official capacity were the same ones having extramarital affairs.

So my mom spent years shoveling shit for the church, and I didn't come out smelling like a rose either. The short of it is that I loved God, and at the same time, despised man's corruption of the God I'd come to know. I was done with the church, eyes wide open to everything I'd witnessed. As a result, I'd made a second adult decision: to create my own path.

But here was this flier for a midnight church service at a music venue. And at the time I came across it, I was stuck between two worlds. I wasn't a drinker and partier like the friends who reserved Saturday nights for getting shit-faced, and I was no longer a churchgoer like others who said their prayers at ten o'clock so they could get a good night's sleep before service on Sunday morning. The few left over were like me: done with traditional church and hungry for something more meaningful than a late-night debate over whether pizza or tacos were the ultimate drunk food.

So my Saturday nights consisted mostly of Showtime at the Apollo. And don't get me wrong, Showtime at the Apollo was the jam. What wasn't the jam, though, was laughing alone at the punchlines I caught during moments of clear TV reception, and wondering about the ones I missed that left the audience draped on the laps of the strangers seated next to them. Bottom line, I was fully awake and fully fucking bored on Saturday nights.

Yes, I had said good riddance to the church. At the same time, I remained a little unsettled, like a guy who cuts ties with his significant other, while still holding out hope that she might realize she's been an asshole and come crawling back. So this, alongside my crippling boredom, was enough to try a church for people like me—night owls who are gearing up when others are winding down. Little did I know, in just a few weeks, my routine of clocking out, chowing down, and picking up my friends for church would lead me like a pig to the slaughter.

Fleeing for My Life

As soon as I saw the shooters, I threw my body down across the middle console and hit the gas like a gazelle being chased by three bloodthirsty lions. Oblivious to what was in front of me, but knowing it was preferable to what was behind, I almost immediately slammed into the curb. It was as if the violent jolt shook me awake, and I was suddenly flooded with awareness of the stark reality of the situation—and a revelation about reality in general.

All at once and despite my panic, I had a vivid realization that there was no right place *and* no wrong place. I was caught in a storm of steel comets hurling towards us at 1,200 feet per second—*nowhere* was safe. A move to the left or to the right was just as likely to put me into the bullet's path as out of it. Duck and maybe the bullet aimed at my shoulder would find my head.

> The violent jolt shook me awake.

At that moment, there was nothing I could do to influence the aim of my shooters, the calibration or caliber of their guns, or whether I or my friends got hit. All I could do was drive like hell and hope that this was the opening act of the rest of my life, not the final scene.

Somehow, all this was rushing through my head with absolute clarity amongst the chaos that was playing out around me.

After I hit the curb, I raised my head just enough to see over the steering wheel, and I sped toward the bridge half a block away as bullets continued to rain down on the vehicle. When we were finally in the clear, I headed straight for the ER at Abbott Northwestern, one of the biggest hospitals in Minnesota that, thank God, was just a few blocks away.

Marcus was shot in the leg that had gotten lodged between the seat and cassette case. He was right in the path of a bullet that would've hit me directly in the chest. I was grazed under the skin of my left eye. Later, I discovered that if my head had been positioned just a few millimeters to either side, the cold steel would've penetrated my skull. My vehicle fared less well. The rear window was blown out and the front one was cracked. Bullets had passed through the dashboard, a tire, the back seat, and the trunk, where one ended up inside my full gas tank. Nevertheless, we'd survived.

Making Sense of the Senseless

When something that senseless happens, it's natural to search for meaning. If you can find answers, maybe you can keep it from happening again. Who were those guys, and why were they shooting at us?

I've been lost in thought many times over the years replaying the events in my head, analyzing, for example, how fast Tyrell had closed the door when he got in. As cunning as Tyrell was in his hustle, something told me he had crossed some motherfuckers you don't cross.

> When something that senseless happens, it's natural to search for meaning.

But I can't prove it. I never found out, and the fact is I'll never know. Besides, what would it accomplish if I did? Maybe that's the way it was meant to be: a senseless and close encounter with death.

I didn't choose this. Who controls whether they're cast into such cruel twists of fate? The person who's hit with a stray bullet in a gunfight between complete strangers as they're walking into the store to pay for gas? What about the one driving home from band practice who collides with the teen driver texting his significant other? And who chooses to develop late-stage cancer? Not my friends whose diagnoses later served as a harsh reminder of the lessons I learned though my brush with death.

When those dark figures approached like the unholy trinity, I was flooded with awareness of my mortality and the weight of the decisions that led to this moment, the potential period at the end of my story.

I realized then that all this religious programming about "God's judgment" might be misdirected. Yes, I did imagine myself standing before my Creator and recounting my life. However, there was something else—something even more unsettling. I felt the crushing weight of *my own* judgment. What I felt about me, my own verdict on the way I had lived, came into sharp focus.

And I realized that the judgment had more to do with what I hadn't done than what I had. What hadn't I reconciled? Or in the words of my religious upbringing, where had I not "repented?" *Yeah, God's gonna judge me*, I thought, *but God can wait because right now, I'm at risk of getting stuck with permanent regrets—regrets I am 100% responsible for causing*. In other words, this wasn't about some outside judge casting a sentence. I was like a kid knowing he'd done wrong and "gotten away with it," only to be left with the unyielding consequence of a guilty conscience.

> I felt the crushing weight of my own judgment.

If you believe in a higher power, maybe you're asking yourself, "What's God going to judge me for?" Well, you might be asking the wrong question. I suspect God is like any loving parent, who wants you to live with a free and loving spirit, not live in fear of their judgment. That's what I think it means to stand before God without shame—loving life and pursuing fulfillment, not fearing death and the judgment that might come with it.

Or maybe you wonder, "What does God think of me?" Well, judge me if you'd like, but I say, fuck that. Start with you—what do you think of yourself? If my brush with death taught me one thing, it's that my opinion of myself matters more than I ever could have imagined. It's the one question I was faced with when my life was hanging on the brink, and I suspect it might be the same for you, whether you believe in God or not—what do I think of myself? Think what you will of God, none of that love is getting through if you hate and disapprove of yourself.

But what do your parents think? What about your boss, your friends, your fitness buddies? How will you be judged by the stranger passing on the street, or better yet the one visiting your social media page?

Relying on others as your moral compass is a waste of energy and time, and both are in limited supply. Instead, receive their feedback, consider how it sits with your gut, and let them think what they think.

We get so caught up asking ourselves what some Higher Power will do with us when we pass on that we neglect to ask ourselves how *we* will judge our life. No one really knows what happens when we die until we get there. The verdict of your conscience, the part of you I believe is imprinted with God's spirit, depends on how you use *now*, not how you performed yesterday and not what you plan on getting around to tomorrow.

> What if we were to live our lives with no fear?

And eventually, whether senseless or not, death just *is*. Aside from the experience of this moment, it's the one thing we all share in common with every other person we encounter. And no matter who you are, how well-behaved, accomplished, or "in control," death doesn't ask for an invitation. When it shows up, it doesn't ask if you have any questions to make sure it all makes sense to you.

There's a paradox in how we go about living. On one hand, we're blissfully ignorant to our ultimate and unplanned expiration. And yet, we live in perpetual fear over bullshit that we have no control over. But what if we were to live our lives with no fear? Not in a reckless way—not "I'm going to die anyway, so fuck it, let's max out the credit cards." No, in a purposeful way, living as if today could be your last, living *because* today might be.

Transforming Setbacks into Significance

You can count on it: life will throw curveballs that are beyond our control, including stark reminders of our mortality. Yet, it's often those moments that initially seem devastating that can shock us into action, steering us toward a life of intentionality, one that honors our personal values and decisions. Our creative power lies in turning challenges into catalysts for a purposeful and self-directed life.

MAKING LIFE DOPE:

As we pivot to this new perspective, grab your Life Is Dope Journal or a piece of paper and take the next few minutes to consider the following:

- If you knew you had just 24 hours left, what actions would you take to create a lasting impact?
    - Think about what you wish to be remembered for and how you can utilize this precious time to live authentically, free of regrets.

- Think about the possibility that this breath could be your last—what regrets surface?
    - What have you delayed that now feels urgent?
    - What words of love, forgiveness, or admiration remain unsaid by you?
- From your reflections, choose one action to take *immediately*. Deadass, before you start the next chapter, before you pee, or before you scroll. Choose something that will propel you toward living a life of intentional significance. This could be as simple as expressing love, starting a long-procrastinated project, or making a decision you've been putting off.

After taking this action, pause and assess how you feel. This moment of reflection is the essence of transforming self-sabotage into significance, of molding a life that is truly dope in every sense—vibrant, meaningful, and driven by your deepest convictions.

BONUS:
Dive deeper by using the official Life Is Dope Accompaniment workbook, music playlists and more for free, by visiting MichaelAnthonyTV.com/LifeIsDope or scanning this QR code:

STORY 2

Act Like an Owner

Come out of the shadow
Step into the light
This could be the moment
It could change your life
—**Lea Michelle, "Louder"**

"Your schedule is more rigid than the monks and nuns in a monastery!"

Well, this was ironic. At their wit's end about the havoc my moral depravity was wreaking on our family, my parents sent me to see this counselor, a former nun, who was now coming to my defense. At seventeen, I was buried under a brutal ministry schedule, squeezing in school, and still felt like I was perpetually falling short of fear-based holiness standards perpetuated by the church and my parents.

> *I internalized all of it. I was a piece of shit, lower than dirt.*

Plus, I had "destroyed" my and my family's lives by becoming sexually involved with a girl. My mom told me under no uncertain terms that I was evil, a "predator" who was hurting women. She went so far as to call my penis evil. My dad, on the other hand, spared me all the preaching and just beat the shit out of me. And I internalized all of it. I was a piece of shit, lower than dirt.

And now, this counselor was encouraging me to stop bending to my parents' impossible standards of piety. Her advice? Get the fuck out.

The Freedom of the Cage

Needless to say, life was pretty shitty at the time. I spent the last few months of high school turned inwards, away from all my friends, and my inner world was no more hospitable than the one outside. Something had to give.

Like I mentioned, the first thing I did upon graduation, on the advice of the rebel nun, was to get a job. Fortunately, I was just a short drive from the largest retail hub in the western hemisphere, the Mall of America, where opportunities were plentiful for seventeen-year-olds. I hoped that my first job peddling shoes at Marshalls would be the introduction to a new chapter of my life.

Eventually, I worked enough hours to afford a third-floor duplex, a nasty bathroom-and-a-half that also happened to be the tutoring center of the now-closed ministry center where I once ran as a volunteer. The carpet there was like a science experiment, and athlete's foot was the subject under study. But that's where I lived because that's what I could afford.

> My inner world was no more hospitable than the one outside.

In hindsight, the early-morning shift at Marshalls from six to two—off the sales floor and away from the shoe department—became an unexpected sanctuary from the storms of my family and church life. It took place in "the cage," a massive fenced-in area underneath the mall where the shipments of merchandise arrived. Being in the cage was more relaxing than working in the store where there was a strict dress code—dress pants, dress shoes, and a light blue button down shirt emblazoned with the Marshalls logo. In the cage, you could wear whatever the heck you wanted.

By the same token, you could get away with far worse behavior there than damn near anywhere else I'd experienced in society to that point. Nothing was sacred, and we clowned all day, every day down there—throwing stock at each other, doing and saying *anything* to get a laugh and lighten the mood of doing the grunt work of the Marshalls operation. Bottom line, nobody gave a crap what the heaven or hell you said, which couldn't have been any different from the buttoned-up formality I was used to.

> They were real people doing their best to get by.

Quite a few of the people I worked with were churchgoers but without the slightest air of sanctimony—they used language as colorful as their personalities and embraced their sexuality without shame or apology. And despite all that, they weren't evil. They weren't "predators" as my mom had called me when I began to explore my sexuality. They were real people doing their best to get by.

That was the beauty of trading the chains of the ministry for the cage of Marshalls. There was no place for that shame in the cage. Here, people loved me for the perfectly broken, Jesus-loving person I was. I didn't have to toe the line to avoid being judged or reprimanded. The early shift provided the ideal indoctrination into what a kid my age was supposed to be doing—working hard, sure, and also fucking around.

Digging Through Rubble

That's when the digging started, scouring through the rubble to find who I was underneath all the shit that had been heaped on top of me. And that's why Marshalls holds a dearer place in my heart than it does for even the most ardent, bargain-hunting, credit-card-toting suburban soccer mom.

Working in the cage, I could talk all the shit that I wanted with my jeans sagged as low as I wanted as long as I got my work done. After years of walking on eggshells and accepting oppression like I deserved it, this was just what the doctor ordered—permission to express myself.

One of the co-workers who impacted me most profoundly in this search was Sarderia, an exceedingly sweet woman in her late thirties and the mom of a teenager and a newborn baby. One day, I was working alongside Sarderia and listening to her talk about her kids when it suddenly dawned on me—*she's earning the same amount of money that I am*. Then I looked over at another co-worker, a grandmother who was working in the cage so she could eat when she should've been kicking up her feet and watching *Judge Judy*. Somehow, I'd overlooked that every one of the beautiful souls in this happily dysfunctional work family of mine were significantly older than me and still at the very bottom of the professional totem pole.

This wasn't about seeing myself as better than them. In fact, it was the opposite. I loved these people. I felt empathy for them. And at the same time, I felt a determination deep in my stomach to not end up with the same fate. I'd come here because I didn't know what I wanted to do with my life. Now, I had a renewed urgency to figure it out. And in order to do that, I had to get honest with myself.

What do I really want to do?

I considered a few of the co-workers who were closer to my age. There was the clean-cut kid from the suburbs who was in college and working here to fund his social life, and the uneducated but street-smart kid here to account for the money he earned through drug-dealing. Then there was the four-foot-tall lady with no college degree and the tenacity of a pit bull who started on the floor like the rest of us and clawed her way to management. Did I want to be like any of them?

Working at Marshalls was comfortable. And yet, I knew full well I didn't want to spend my entire life living from paycheck to paycheck and meal to meal. I'd watched my dad deliver pizzas on top of a full-time job and still have to borrow money from his sister. At one point, we had to break into our own house to get our stuff after the locks were changed during its foreclosure. My parents gave me an invaluable financial education on how bad shit could be, and I wanted the opposite.

Even at seventeen, I had dreams of becoming financially independent, even a millionaire. Unless I was going to abandon that dream, I realized I'd have to take an honest look at what I was doing and ask, "Is this going to get me where I want to be?" I needed to start looking ahead to the vehicle that was going to get me there, and my old rundown Cutlass, fueled by my Marshalls paychecks, wasn't gonna cut it.

Owning My Destiny

I knew I was an outlier. I'd always been an outlier. For one, I didn't speak like I do now. Where I grew up, speaking proper English was an invitation for harassment at best and a death wish at worst. Consequently, I talked more like Dr. Dre than Dr. Phil, and my pants were baggy enough to fit two legs in each hole and saggy enough to leave no question of what kind of drawers I was wearing underneath. Don't get it twisted, though—I loved it. This was *my* lifestyle forged from the world I lived in.

My parents gave me an invaluable financial education on how bad shit could be.

Up to that point, I was not willing to change any of this. In fact, I just considered it my identity. But I had to face that there were parts of my so-called identity that had worked where I'd been, but not where I wanted to go. Of course, I didn't want to sell out to the rich, snooty folks. At the same time, I had to consider the possibility that the whole idea of "selling out" was bullshit. And maybe my aversion to it was actually self-sabotage.

So seeing the writing on the wall, I chose to be honest with myself—changing the trajectory of my life would require changing some aspects of my identity that were no longer serving me. That didn't mean I had to become a different person. It just meant I had to step back and consider a different way of being that I could live with. Even if it wasn't comfortable at first, I had to start becoming someone in charge of his destiny.

Of course, I had some hangups. There was an aspect of talking like the middle class and rich folks I grew up making fun of that I had fundamental issues with, some of which I still relate to. I felt like I was betraying myself and everything I grew up standing for.

But now I was asking myself, *Is this really about behaving like a certain class? Will I be selling out by adjusting the way I dress and walk to get where I want to be?* I realized I had to do what was necessary to claim ownership over my life and my destiny. If "keeping it real" was standing in the way of my progress, I had to decide which to prioritize—my pride or my future. It was time to get out of my comfort zone and assimilate into the universal culture of professionalism and affluence.

> I chose to be honest with myself.

Loving What Is

I wanted to become a millionaire. I also wanted to wake up whenever I wanted to. I'm not a 5:00 a.m.'er. Well, guess what? I wasn't a millionaire yet, and work in the cage started at 6:00 a.m. So I got my ass up at 5:00 a.m, pulled on my giant jeans and went to work.

In the same way, I've been through seasons when I had to get up at 4:45 a.m. to hit the gym before I went to work. Why? Because that's the identity I chose for that season. I decided *I want this, so I will be the person who does this.*

The same thing applies to whatever is necessary to get what you want for yourself. If your identity is not getting your ass up out of bed, but what you desire in your life demands it, well, one's gotta go.

Now, I'm at a point in my life, where I pretty much get up when I want to, talk how I want to, dress how I want to, and go where I want to. I've come a long way from that seventeen-year-old kid in baggy jeans and an accent that seemed out-of-place anywhere outside the hood. And I got there by taking ownership over my life, even when it meant doing things I "didn't want to do." And it all started with a decision at seventeen to take control of how others perceived me in order to achieve what I wanted.

I left the mindset of the teenager behind—the mindset of the kid who says, "Fuck you, I don't need you anyway" or "Fuck that, I won't do what you tell me to do," then goes home and blames the world because he can't get anywhere in life. Well, yeah, a stubborn insistence to stay the same ensures just that.

If you're saying, "This is who I am!" and not getting the result you desire, then it might be beneficial to ask yourself, That's the work that started in me the day I decided to make and live by my own standards, instead of fighting the losing battle of trying to be what others wanted. That's a battle where even the "wins" cost you, depleting your spirit because the victories aren't your own.

If you want to make a positive change, whether it's shifting your mindset or getting a new job, start giving yourself tough love and doing the work required to make that change. That's not shaming—that's having the guts to acknowledge that most people who are out-of-shape and working at dead-end jobs aren't happy to be the way they are.

To love yourself, you also have to love the sacrifices necessary to get what you deeply desire. Far more of our pain comes from loving what we want rather than loving what is. Thinking, "I want to do whatever I want, AND I want to earn X amount" is like saying, "I want to eat whatever I want, and I want to lose weight." Or, "I want to be undisciplined, and I want to be wealthy." Well, good luck with that! Prepare for a hell of a lot more pain than if you'd accepted the reality of what it takes to get what you want. That's loving what is.

What do you want? What do you really want? Do you want to be wealthy? Then love the reality. Love what is, on the way to what will be. You have to work your way into a field where there is money to be made, and you have to exercise discipline when you get there. You gotta live on less than you make. Period. Love the reality of what it takes to achieve what you want. Of course you want to do what you love and make money, too—who the fuck doesn't? If you're lucky enough to find both, great! If not, then choose which matters more and learn to love the necessary sacrifice. Save yourself the mess of pissing in the wind.

The Gift of Adversity

"Mike, the challenge you have in life is that you were given the hard card, not the easy one," my mentor, Dan, once said to me. "Your gift and opportunity is to work through all of it and become a better person as a result—a more developed person, a more developed leader, someone who ends up stronger and more successful than the average person."

> *You gotta live on less than you make. Period.*

When you're dealt a bad hand or even a bad card, it gives credence to the illusion that power lies outside of you, beyond your control. It makes your happiness and success contingent upon other people and circumstances. It's a recipe for helplessness and resentment.

I had obstacles. I wasn't just carrying my trauma, but the trauma that my parents and my parents' parents failed to address. And let's face it—my skin color and gender gave me a leg up when I decided to change my speech and my behaviors to match it. In other words, I wasn't dealing with some of the obstacles that others are born into.

There may well be men trying to hold you back on the basis of your gender. You might be being treated unfairly because of your ethnicity. You might have some handicap that hinders your options and progress. The unfortunate reality is that we're never going to completely get rid of discrimination, and there are some things each of us aren't cut out for. Anyone who's ever heard me attempt karaoke knows I won't be a professional singer.

> *Be too focused on your vision to waste energy on the ones who can't or won't see it.*

It's *not* fair. And yet, this is where a good dose of "fuck off" is in order. If someone can't get over the fact you have a vagina or a different skin color, they're not worthy of you. I'm not talking about having resentment, but indifference. Your worthiness—your ability to become a better and stronger person—does not depend on approval. You decide what and who is worthy of your time. That is the gift endowed to everyone at birth, regardless of race, gender, or handicap.

The power question for me and you is, *will I let the past dictate the future?* Am I going to rail against how unfair things are, or am I going to transform the anger, hurt, and rage into fuel for my future success?

Honestly, I had to give up some parts of my identity to move forward. Hell, I had to talk like a suburbanite—because I realized that by "sticking it to society," I was actually sabotaging my future.

Now more than ever, people love the sound of their own bitching and complaining. Sure, some of it's justified, but ask yourself this: how does dwelling on the challenge and injustice help you? The fact is, you can focus on judging and comparing yourself to the other, more-fortunate person, or you can focus on improving the *only* one whose actions and fate you have any direct control over—you.

Because one thing is for certain—you're going to get shit on from every direction at some point in time. So, be so bold and beautiful and great at what you do, that all of that shit slides away like water off a duck's back. Be too focused on your vision to waste energy on the ones who can't or won't see it.

If you keep your head down and concentrate on leveling up, someday you'll look around and think, "I'll be damned, I'm the HBIC." (For those who don't know, that's *Head Bitch In Charge.*) That's the person in the position to do something about the things everybody else just bitches about. And when you get there, you'll have the opportunity to extend grace and compassion to the ignorant, knowing what a sad way of life they lead, and give inspiration to those determined to grow through the harshest of conditions.

So what's holding you back? What are you willing to let go of to become who you desire to be? You don't have to deny the injustice. Own it. Use your resources to enact change. Make the culture better. Nothing is impossible to the person who believes they have ultimate ownership over their life, and you are the owner.

> *One thing remains irrevocably yours: your ability to choose a dream that's worth the pain.*

So whatever color you are, whatever gender you are, however you walk or talk or dress, become so fucking good at what you choose to do that they have no choice but to take notice and wish they had you on their team. That is the gift you can give to yourself—the gift of choosing strength that defies oppression.

Claiming Ownership of Your Journey

Claiming ownership involves embracing a couple of life's truths: nothing will be handed to you, and you can count on life not being fair. As bleak as this may sound, there's a profound empowerment in realizing that one thing remains irrevocably yours: your ability to choose a dream that's worth the pain.

Take an honest look at the persona you're cultivating. Are you confusing behaviors you've learned with who you are? And what are the costs of that in the way you relate to yourself, others, and the world?

As you reflect deeply on your desires and the responsibility to act that lies with you, remember that life is not about waiting for opportunities to land in your lap. It's about making bold choices, seizing control, and transforming adversity into growth and self-doubt into a narrative of triumph.

You're the architect of your reality, the author of your life story. So, no matter your background or circumstances, it's within your power to excel in your chosen path so remarkably that the world takes notice. Embrace the incredible gift of self-determination, and use it to carve out a life of significance. That's the true essence of living the dope life.

MAKING LIFE DOPE:

Now, I want you to grab your Life is Dope journal or Workbook and consider the following:

- Reflect on your current life situation…
    - In which areas of your life are you not accepting "what is"?
    - Where are you wasting energy wishing things outside your control were different?
    - Are there issues you're ignoring, effectively approving their existence through your inaction?
- Focus on what you control…
    - What aspects of your life that you wish were different and have the power to change…
    - What's ONE thing you can do, however small, to initiate change?
    - If you're hesitant to take even a small step, what's the fear that's holding you back?
- Evaluate your career and work…
    - Are your current job and career path leading you to where you truly want to be?
    - If not, consider what steps will help you, whether it's gaining new skills over the next six months or making a more immediate change.

> *You're the architect of your reality.*

Turn your focus toward the parts of your life that you wish were different *and* have the power to change. If you're really not willing to take that one step, then respectfully and for your own good, it's time to confront why and how you can move past that resistance.

BONUS:

Dive deeper by using the official Life Is Dope Accompaniment workbook, music playlists and more for free, by visiting MichaelAnthonyTV.com/LifeIsDope or scanning this QR code:

STORY 3

You're Meant for More

What doesn't kill you makes you stronger, stand a little taller
Doesn't mean I'm lonely when I'm alone
What doesn't kill you makes a fighter, footsteps even lighter
—**Kelly Clarkson, "Stronger**
(What Doesn't Kill You) Promise Land Remix"

Believe it or not, my brush with death en route to the midnight service didn't scare me away from church. Instead, it set off a chain reaction.

By age twenty, I had a job at the same Christian music club we were heading to when our drive was interrupted by a chorus of gunfire. And I was damn good at what I did there—I started off managing the production department, and by the time I left, I was practically running the place like a GM and concert promoter.

But what was the financial payoff for the grueling ninety-plus-hour workweeks during this period of personal development? Something in the neighborhood of jack squat.

And I wasn't only hustling for myself, I'd met a woman, Sarah. And a few months later, on a mission trip to Peru, I popped the question. (Spoiler: she said yes). Five years after that, we welcomed our firstborn, a daughter.

Meanwhile, I was "doing the work of the Lord," putting on live music events for an income so low that at one point we qualified for food stamps.

Sarah and I lived in a neighborhood dubbed "Phillips," a name the city invented to distract from its real identity—the ghetto. There was a playground a couple of blocks from our house where you wouldn't send your kids unless they were helping you run crack or clean up dirty needles as community service.

During that season, Sarah would sometimes drive fifteen blocks down the road to a fancy grocery store in Uptown for a vacation from the squalor. She always came back from these outings refreshed, like she'd been cleansed of the muck of the inner city and hopeful that we might someday find our way out of it for good. But one day, a couple hours after she had departed for her getaway, she called me crying hysterically.

She'd decided just this once to buy a gallon of milk for our daughter, and the moment the cashier saw her EBT card, she barked out, "We don't take food stamps!"

Seeing this all go down, the angel of a woman who happened to be next in line sprung to pay for our groceries. This resolved the immediate crisis but not the humiliation Sarah felt at being exposed as a person who lived on the wrong side of town.

Sarah is my best friend. She believed in me then just as much as she does now. She's also a hustler, a woman who cuts through the bullshit, shows up and does what's necessary. And as any provider worth their salt can tell you, there's no greater pain than failing to meet the needs of a partner like that, much less subjecting them to public shaming when they go to escape the sad reality of your shared life.

Flavor of Inspiration

I'd failed. This wasn't supposed to be some seasonal thing—I'd planned to do this for life. My intention in taking on this spiritual vocation was to please God and make a healthy living. It seemed as though I'd fallen short on both.

> I'd failed.

Despite it all, I'd been doing my best to hold it together, tell myself, *It's okay... EVERYTHING'S OKAY!* But in the heart of this perceived failure, a seed of truth began to sprout: maybe I *wasn't* okay. It was the first, faltering step toward acknowledging the whisper of a promise that I was meant for more.

Still, I had a long way to go. Completely fucked in the head and in no place to step up to the plate for Sarah, I wrestled with shame—torn between leaving the ministry and the fear of falling short in providing for my family. To make matters worse, my mentors warned me: "Leave the ministry, and you'll be walking out of God's will."

> *When well-intended leaders misguide in the name of God, people get hurt.*

When well-intended leaders misguide in the name of God, people get hurt. Looking back, I realize the absurdity of believing that God would want me to suffer. At the time, though, I was the perfect target for this sort of spiritual gaslighting. It's no exaggeration to say that I feared that God might strike me with lightning if I left to support my family and prioritize my health. So I suffered silently, feeling afraid to admit it, let alone embrace the vulnerability needed to move beyond it. *I was okay.*

Nevertheless, the seeds of discontent were fully sewn, and my misery had reached a point where I was willing to risk my soul to save my life. It was time to call the bluff on my fear, betting that whatever spanking I got for leaving the ministry would be preferable to the hell I was dragging my family through.

So after five years in ministry, I left the church job and found a sales job with a company that printed the packaging for CDs and DVDs.

I hit the ground running, determined to plow my way out of poverty for the sake of my family. Right out of the gate, I learned from the powers-that-be exactly how much I would need to sell to bring in the six-figure income that I'd once believed I could earn doing all the "right things" for the church.

Well, the answer turned out to be *a shitload*—I'd need to build a million dollar book of businesses in my first year. Meanwhile, my buddy Dr. Tony Shore, who was with the company, had already signed on with every potential lead I had in the industry.

No worries. I had the rest of the industry guidebook to work with, and I started cold-calling, from "J" to "Z"—I figured *somebody* had done this before, but they probably started with "A!" I had a plan and hustled like my life depended on it. After all, I'd "forsaken God" for this, so maybe it did.

In the end, I hit my mark, concluding my first year with a million-dollar book of business, which included an account with the largest indie rock label in the industry. (Shoutout to Clint at Victory for giving me a shot!)

> I had a plan and hustled like my life depended on it.

And in return, I earned *not* six figures…but forty-thousand dollars. The people in charge of overseeing the budgeting and overall profitability of the printing department were salaried—they didn't care about profitability. As a result, the commissions paid didn't match the promises made by the company.

This was not working. I'd taken a leap of faith—away from the faith—and ended up slamming into rock bottom.

I'm okay. It's going to be okay.

Completely deflated and lost about what to do next, divine inspiration came not from God, but Flavor Flav. Yes, the founding member and hype man to the legendary hip-hop group Public Enemy. Reality TV was in its infancy at the time, and my vice was the train wreck known as *Flavor of Love*, a show in which contestants competed for the hand of Flav.

There was something hypnotic about watching these C-list celebrities destroy their lives, not by smoking crack or sharing needles, but by making a complete mockery of their highest selves. With all its blatant debauchery and petty drama, this show was all about playing to the lowest denominator. It was bizarre, to say the least… and I ate it up.

Until one day, through the stupor of *Flavor of Love*, it hit me. I'm over here fighting with all I have to make a better life for me and my family, busting my ass every day at work, while these motherfuckers ride this shitshow all the way to the bank.

> Now that I could see where I was, it was time to make a major change.

And just like that, I went from telling myself, *I'm okay. It's going to be okay—just keep going*, to being fed up and unwilling to proceed. I'd been putting all of my faith in circumstances I couldn't control and waiting for someone to see my efforts and make a way for me. Suddenly the whisper became a shout: *You are meant for MORE!*

It was as if the "Your Location" dot on the GPS screen of my life had just appeared, revealing that I was nowhere near where I wanted to be. And now that I could see where I was, it was time to make a major change. A change that waited on no one's permission. This town had been beating me down for twenty-eight years and showed no sign of letting up. I needed to get the fuck out of Minneapolis.

Hope Against Hope

Old habits die hard. I knew it was time for a change, I knew I was capable of more, but what now?

I watched as the familiar patterns of thinking crept back in. *Why me? Why is all of this happening? Can I catch a mother fucking break?*

By this time, we'd adopted our son, going from a family of three to a family of four. The timing couldn't have been worse to realize the job I'd hung my hopes on had been oversold. I was almost completely consumed with frustration and discouragement—*almost*.

Despite it all, that flicker of hope that visited me through trash TV kept hanging around, refusing to be extinguished. It was strange. Despite feeling utterly beat down, I had this inexplicable sense that something big was around the corner. A few days later, I said as much to my close friend and workout buddy, Mark.

"I don't know what's coming," I said, "but I feel this huge change coming. I'm excited." Maybe I was about to land some big account that I had been working towards with the print company. Maybe there was a new job prospect on the horizon. I had no idea, but the thrill of the unknown propelled me forward.

> The thrill of the unknown propelled me forward.

Two days later, I left for a week-long business trip to Nashville. From my first encounter with my friend JR at the Tin Roof 2 in Cool Springs to my final chat with Bob Goldstein over a meal in a little hole-in-the-wall restaurant downtown—where he'd sell me on the appeal of sushi—one message rang clear: everyone I met, in *all ten* of my meetings, couldn't stop raving about life in Nashville or urging me to move there.

None of these motherfuckers knew each other. None knew that I didn't have any particular liking for Nashville and certainly no inkling to live there. And yet, every meeting intended for pitching our print services to clients turned into clients pitching Nashville to me. It was too bizarre to be chalked up to chance.

Emboldened by this series of serendipitous encounters and the lingering inspiration of Flavor Flav, the pull towards that vague sense of *more* became stronger than ever. There was no telling myself *I'm okay*. Something had to give.

Dumbfounded by what I'd experienced over the course of the week, I called Sarah with the intention of laying my feelings, however irrational, out in the open. I didn't want to explain things away, and I didn't want to leave open the possibility of regret.

"Hey, this may sound crazy, but I just gotta throw it out there," I said. "What would you think if, hypothetically, one day we were to move to Nashville." And without skipping a beat, she answered. "That sounds great. I've been waiting for you to say something for a year."

That was October. I returned home, and we started to deal with the reality of the situation. What's the plan? We had two cars, only one fit to make the fifteen-hour trek to Nashville. We owned a brownstone coop that we'd have to sell at a time when the Minnesota housing market was taking a nosedive—a downturn the rest of the country would soon follow. And how would I make money once I got there? Money was tight as it was.

Despite all our questions and reservations, we followed our gut: I'd move to Nashville in three months for the beginning of the new year.

The pressure was on.

I knew that I'd have to make some moves if I was going to make this happen. I needed money. More money than I could make finding clients for the print company. I had a couple of weeks' salary in PTO I could cash in. I had a moped I used to commute to work I could sell for a few hundred bucks and some DJ equipment worth a decent chunk of change.

When all was said and done, through sheer determination to rise above our circumstances, I saved up eighteen hundred dollars, enough for a couple of months of rent. Sarah had a few hundred more to cover utilities and food. And mercifully, I had two generous friends, Brenda and Doug Price, who forever changed the course of my life when they let me stay rent free in Spring Hill, on a street called, of all things, Faith Lane! I had five months, six at most to get my shit together and lay a foundation in Nashville that was solid enough for my family to build upon.

Choosing to embrace this new direction did not erase the trials that preceded it. The shadows of doubt and defeat lingered, a stark reminder of the hurdles I'd overcome. Yet, this very vulnerability, the willingness to face my fears and act despite them, paved the way for genuine transformation. It underscored the power of hope against hope, the courage to pursue authenticity, and the conviction that, indeed, I was meant for more. As I prepared to leave Minneapolis behind, it wasn't just a relocation—I was embarking on a profound journey toward realizing my true potential.

> I am meant for more.

Now, my actions were doing the talking: *I am meant for more.*

Standing on the Brink

Only after I'd packed what few belongings I could fit into my car did I take a minute to breathe and ponder what was ahead. I stood alone at the bay windows of the third-floor guest room, the familiar Minneapolis skyline stretching out before me.

This place was all I'd known since I moved here as a four-year-old boy with his fresh-out-of-rehab mom. Where I learned everything I knew about life. Every friend, every memory was anchored here. And after more than two decades, what did I have to show for it?

I was a failed minister, a disgruntled salesman, and an insufficient provider. A father of two innocent children who depended on me to support and guide them. A husband to a fearlessly-loving woman who believed in me enough to follow me halfway across the country. Meanwhile, the mind of the person they were counting on was a mess, exploding with thought after thought and question after question, each more unconstructive than the last: *What are you thinking? This is dumb. You're insane. Don't fucking move!*

Was I divinely guided or supremely delusional? I wasn't sure. Nevertheless, I was faced with two options: follow my gut and risk failure or remain in Minneapolis and die inside.

Looking out the window, bathed in the warm glow of the room with its orange-tinged walls, I felt profoundly afraid and alone. And then, against the backdrop of the night, I caught a glimpse of my reflection staring back at me from the frost-kissed glass.

I saw a broken man, eyes flooded with tears, hands balled tight, ready to punch the window in frustration at his lot in life—years of sexual abuse, physical abuse, verbal abuse, years of manipulation and deceit in the ministry and the workplace alike. I realized I didn't love the person staring back at me. I was ashamed of him, and I didn't know how to fix him.

> I saw a broken man, eyes flooded with tears.

Then, from the center of my desperation came an answer, a quiet certainty that cut through the noise of my frantic doubts and questions. It was somehow familiar, gentle but resolute and bathed in wisdom and grace. Was it me? Was it God? I didn't know. I still don't. But the message was clear.

You're meant for more.

MAKING LIFE DOPE:

Before we move forward, I want you to take a moment and reflect:

- Get out your Life Is Dope journal or workbook and write: "I am meant for more." Sit with that for a bit.
  - What does "You are meant for more" mean for you? Write down the first thing that comes to mind with minimal thought and reflection.
  - Where are you experiencing less than what's in your heart because of BS excuses you're accepting as truth?
- If you find yourself stuck on what "more" means to you, set a timer for 90 seconds, and start by writing, "I am meant for more. I am meant for ___." In other words, what is the "more" that's yours to pursue?
- If you stay stuck, just keep writing "I am meant for more" until something else comes to you. The key is to write *nonstop* and keep repeating it until something more surfaces from within. This exercise, called "free form writing," isn't just about affirming your potential; it's about excavating your unacknowledged thoughts and emotions to find what that "more" truly means for you.

Remember: the "winning" I'm experiencing today is because of seeds that were planted in faith, in that ground fertilized from hardship that even I often overlooked. I am the product of all of my hardship, and I am wildly grateful for where I am, who I have become, and who I am becoming.

So, as you continue through the pages of this book, remember that the trials and tribulations you've faced, the challenges that have tested your resilience, were not in vain. And when doubt creeps in, remind yourself: I am meant for more.

You are destined for greatness, a greatness as distinct as you. Your hardships have planted the seeds of your greatness, and the world eagerly awaits the beauty that will bloom from your journey. When doubt creeps in, remind yourself: *I am meant for more. I am destined for the dope life.*

> You are destined for greatness, a greatness as distinct as you.

DON'T MISS OUT:

Dive deeper by using the official Life Is Dope Accompaniment workbook, music playlists and more for free, by visiting MichaelAnthonyTV.com/LifeIsDope or scanning this QR code:

STORY 4

Success Comes to Those Who Persevere

> God'll take you through hell just to get you to heaven...
> I hope the picture painted clear
> If ya heart filled with faith then ya can't fear
> —**T.I., "No Matter What"**

> You better work, bitch, you better work, bitch...
> Now get to work, bitch!
> **Britney Spears, "Work Bitch"**

On the surface, what I was doing didn't make any sense. I had almost no money and no real plan—only faith in the pit of my belly that Nashville was a place where a reject like me might blaze his own entrepreneurial path.

I was born for more.

> On the surface, what I was doing didn't make any sense.

Or at least that's the thought that sent me packing. But what if I wasn't? What if these first twenty-eight years of shit were just laying the groundwork for a bigger towering pile?

There was an irony to this particular destination that was hard for me to ignore. I loved music, but I really didn't want to work in the industry anymore. I'd been down that road—music made up the majority of my resume, I was burned out on it, and the universe was leading me to... *Music City*?

It felt like a joke—until I got a call from a friend and owner of a Christian artist management company. They had a job opening, and it sounded like it had been written for me by God herself.

The company was home to one of the most well-known artists in the industry as well as a roster of up-and-comers. On top of that, the pay was good with the potential to become great.

The fact that I had an existing relationship with the managers and had even worked with some of their artists was the cherry on top. They understood my business mind and assured me that there was potential for me to have partial ownership as I brought on artists and added value to the company. Hell, I loved them and they loved me back.

This was *it*. I'd come to Nashville in hopes of making it as an entrepreneur, and this felt like God's high-five.

So just like that, I went from full of despair and out of ideas to full of hope and dreaming of all that was to come. Even the rumbling in my belly felt like an omen of future steak dinners. I'd walk around the neighborhood where I was staying rent-free with my friends and look at houses thinking, "Holy shit, I'll actually be able to afford a house down here and lead a normal, comfortable life."

> I went from full of despair and out of ideas to full of hope and dreaming.

And then I got the call. Answering the phone, I lunged in for that celebratory high-five, but instead, God pulled a "Psych!" and jerked his hand, sending my momentum stumbling forward.

The job wasn't going to work out—the top money-making artist of the management company wanted to hire a friend, and when you're managing stars, you do whatever is necessary to keep them happy.

Sometimes hope can turn out to be the most ruthless bitch on earth. I was gutted. Utterly defeated. I felt like a tool, a joke, a complete fucking waste of space. My life was one continuous punchline of failures and rugs pulled out from under my silly ass.

This might have been more manageable if it were just me. I couldn't even take care of myself, so how the hell could I take care of anyone else? I was letting down the woman who had chosen me, and my kids who had no choice who they drew in the dad lotto.

I was seven states away, my body aching, and my head in a vice from barely eating. It seemed that things couldn't get any worse.

> Hope can turn out to be the most ruthless bitch on earth.

I was ready to give up.

A Message in the Storm

In the midst of this roller coaster of events, I made arrangements to meet with Shane Boyd, a veteran in the radio promotion world and a person who could get a laugh out of me no matter how dire my life circumstances. I'd set up the meeting before the artist management job fell through, when I still had some hope left. It seemed things couldn't get any worse… until they did.

On the way to meet Shane, I got a call from Sarah. Before I left Minneapolis, we'd scraped together seven hundred dollars to buy Sarah a minivan off Craigslist so she could comfortably accommodate our one and three-year-old. On the phone, Sarah told me that during rush hour, the "new" minivan had died on Lyndale Avenue, a major throughway in South Minneapolis. She had to get out and push the car alone, crossing two lanes of traffic to reach the slushy shoulder, with the kids sitting inside.

Now here I was, watching the rain hammering the windshield of the car I had committed to selling if I hadn't found a job before the next payment was due. Well, it had been almost a month. I was going to have to sell the car.

Outside, it was the worst kind of Tennessee day: buckets of frigid rain and violent winds, like blasts from an industrial fan. I was also starving, living a lesson that will not appear in any chapter: *fifty cents of food a day will not sustain human life*. When I see pictures of me during that time, I look like I'm on death's door: sunken cheeks and vacant eyes, body laid so bare you could count my ribs.

I'd been giving it absolutely all I had and was left with the feeling that my best was not enough. In other words, *I* was a failure, a deadbeat loser who proved it with every botched attempt at becoming more than that. At least, that's where all signs pointed. I had pursued every known contact, and they all led to dead ends. Either nothing was available, or their offer would put me back in the position of working my ass off for less than my family could live on.

And here I was in Nashville, sitting in a car I needed to sell, waiting to have a meal I didn't have the money to pay for.

I thought, *Be positive. Have gratitude. Be graceful. I am going to deliver so much fucking value to my buddy. Just get water. I'm ok, I already ate. Don't make it weird.*

The last part took precedence. I was 100% committed to that. I wanted to make damn sure he didn't know how much I was dealing with. I didn't want to let on that I was broke. God knows I could've used some charity, but I was defiant about being anyone's charity case.

That tired old script slunk out from its hiding place: *I'M OKAY!*

That's when it occurred to me: *If I start driving now, I could be home by early morning. The interstate's right there—just drive away, Mike! Go back to your family, ashamed and defeated, and find a fucking job—anywhere.*

In a state of desperation, my body primed for fight-or-flight and my mind screamed, "Flight!" I pleaded with God, with the universe, with anyone who would listen, *Why am I such a fucking loser? How do I move forward? How do I come out of this victorious? If I stay, I'm failing. If I go back, I'm a loser. What do I do?*

Then, at that moment, with accusations attacking me from every corner of my conscience, a message took over my being: "Mike, success comes to those who persevere."

The world froze, as if the one speaking was checking to make sure I was listening. And when it was clear that I was, I heard the rest: "Success comes to those who persevere…long enough to *take* it!"

A Decent Meal

As you've probably guessed, I decided to forego the drive and go through with the meeting. And after Shane had ordered his food, the waitress asked what I would like. "Oh, I'm good with just water," I answered with a smile just as I'd rehearsed. I'd barely finished the words when Shane's menu came flying across the table. "The hell you are!" he said. "Mike, you're eating something!" I stuck to my guns. "Really, I'm good." But he wasn't about to accept it. "*Eat.*"

I caved. Shane bought my meal, and to this day, I've never asked what was going through his mind when he undermined my attempt to undermine myself. Maybe he could see that I was wasting away. Maybe that was his unspoken form of charity.

I don't recall what I ate that day, but I do recall a feeling of deep gratitude that Shane refused to relent to my pride. It probably cost him fifteen bucks—a small gesture to him—but it impacted me deeply, and here's why.

I had been persevering and persevering and persevering, and I was about to throw in the towel. I wanted someone to give me an out, to tell me I could quit. Well, that's not what I got. Instead, I got the opposite, and somehow, that refreshed my spirit the second I heard it.

The cavalry wasn't coming. *Nobody* was coming to rescue me.

I walked into the meeting with Shane with a completely different mindset than I'd had before. Sitting across from him, something clicked. I was put firmly in my place, and that place was at the helm of my own life, not passively waiting for a destination. The self-pity that had been consuming me was replaced with a quiet resolve. I'd walked in, determined to hide my shame. Now suddenly, there was no shame left to hide. I didn't need Shane or anyone else to lift me out of my despair. Success was mine to take.

In that moment, a profound realization struck me: *I'm not a victim—I'm a creator.*

> I'm not a victim—
> I'm a creator.

Right there and then, I stopped looking back. I committed to persevere until I could *take* success. And now, savoring the first decent meal I'd had in a long while, I had another sign to keep pushing forward. This wasn't just a meal—it was a symbol of my newfound determination.

The Challenge and Reward of Perseverance

I'd like to tell you my circumstances shifted quickly after that. Far from it. What did shift, though, was my mindset. There would be no more waiting. It was time to seize a better fate, no matter the path I had to take.

Action begets action. That became my guiding principle in the season to come. I'd take any job that got me moving, even the "dead end" job that most people pass up. That job would lead to another and another until I got where—and became who—I desired to be.

> Action begets action.

So I got to work, applying to every legitimate job I could track down while surviving on a five-dollars-per-week food budget. Eventually, I found one. For three weeks, until it went out of business, I washed dishes for eight bucks an hour at a little mom-and-pop Italian restaurant called Sopranoz—not exactly the big opportunity I'd moved halfway across the country to pursue. But that didn't matter. I may have been just sixty-two dollars richer than when I had started, but I was off to the races.

So why do you have to take success? Why doesn't it come easily? Because success is the fairest maiden. She won't lower her standards. She won't respond to self-pity. She won't be taken for granted or settle for mediocrity. She values persistent action fueled by conviction. She seeks only those who likewise recognize their own worth, those ready to be the champions of their destiny.

There's no easy road—success is hard to get and just as hard to keep. And no one's going to hand it to you. Action begets action. When success calls for you, you must have persevered long enough to be ready to grab ahold of it and never let go!

MAKING LIFE DOPE:

Now grab your Life Is Dope journal or workbook and consider the following before proceeding any further:

- Toss aside self-pity and ego. Say to yourself, "I am the author of my life. I have the final say."
    - How do you feel inside when you say this? Does your shoulder or neck tense up? Does your mind shout "Bullshit"? Do you feel peace?
- What's one area where the "college try" is undermining your journey? How does life look differently by removing "trying" and committing to give 100% of who you are?
- What's one challenge in your life right now that could serve as an opportunity for growth and hope instead of failure and pain?
- Does the idea of feedback feel more like personal criticism?

- Think of a recent time when this occurred. How would your life look differently if you viewed this as an opportunity to gain new perspectives, learn and grow?

Remember, success shows up when owning our life is the default. It wasn't enough for me to move to Nashville or to go through the motions of reaching out to people and meeting people with the lukewarm intention of giving it the old college try.

Fuck the college try. Colleges make their money off kids taking six years to finish because of their half-assed attempts to get a four-year degree. In other words, the college try's a college failure. Trying is preparing to fail. It's committing to mediocrity before you've even started.

If my story had ended in that parking lot, at the crossroads of defeat and perseverance, I would be a failure. But deep down, I knew the story wasn't meant to end there. In the same way, your story doesn't end with the challenges or doubts. Like mine, your story begins with each act of perseverance.

BONUS:

Dive deeper by using the official Life Is Dope Accompaniment workbook, music playlists and more for free, by visiting MichaelAnthonyTV.com/LifeIsDope or scanning this QR code:

STORY 5

Flip the Coin

> *One day while my light is glowin'*
> *I'll be in my castle golden*
> *But until the gates are open*
> *I just wanna feel this moment*
> **—Pitbull and Christina Aguilera, "Feel This Moment"**

After a string of jobs that included working in the tasting room at a friend's vineyard (where, ironically, I tasted the first drop of alcohol in my life) and a commissions-only sales job in the most toxic work environment I'd ever been a part of, I finally stumbled upon a job listing that seemed like my ticket out of professional purgatory.

> This was a chance to be a part of something big.

I saw this as my shot at joining the major leagues after years of playing pick-up games—a well-known venture spearheaded by a larger-than-life personality. The company specialized in financial advice and personal development and had a fiercely loyal audience who clung to the founder's every word. They were renowned for their impactful courses, bestselling books, and radio show where the leader shared insights that changed the lives of the audience. This was a chance to be a part of something big.

In the summer of '09, after a *nine*-month hiring process, I got the job. This was it. I was finally making my way out of a cycle of life that had left me financially and spiritually broke.

During the hiring process, though, there were some confusing moments. I noticed more than a few ambiguous utterances and empty reassurances that seemed antithetical to the principles the brand projected. Also, I was starting on entry-level pay— $30,000—which was enough to keep my head close enough to the surface to come up for the occasional gasp of air.

Nevertheless, I was sure my ability to tread water with a smile on my face would double my pay in a year and eventually result in the salary necessary to cruise along in a yacht. *I'm okay. It's going to be okay.*

Do I even have to tell you what happened as I worked my ass off?

Everything went as planned except for the part I never had control over: the payoff. At the end of a year of dedicated work and endless travel, I got a 10% raise, which took me from barely scraping by to, well, still barely scraping by.

> *I'm okay. It's going to be okay.*

At this point, I was like Clark Griswold in *Christmas Vacation*, except he was dreaming of building a swimming pool for his family with his handsome bonus, and I just wanted to turn our AC on. In retrospect, it's fortunate I didn't have a Cousin Eddie around to kidnap the boss.

But really, the problem wasn't with this company. The problem was my skewed perception of corporate America, something I had minimal experience with at the time. I took the job motivated by some pie-in-the-sky ambitions, envisioning a role that would catapult me into the same stratosphere as the founder. More specifically, my focus was narrowed to one grievance: "I'm not being paid enough."

That was all I could see. And because of that, I was oblivious to the other side of this coin—my obsession with money was pickpocketing me of all the joy and opportunity this season had to offer.

A Wake-Up Call

There was a giant juicy carrot dangled in front of me the day I was hired. At least that's the way I saw it. Sure, I'd be scraping by for a while, but if I proved that I could toe the line and walk the walk, they'd take good care of me.

Well, it turned out that there was a massive gap between the hiring manager's idea of "take good care of you" and mine. Raises came in percent increases. Sounds good, right? It did to me when I got hired. What I wasn't accounting for at the time, though, was that 10% of $30,000 dollars for a year of hard work ain't shit, especially when you're the only breadwinner in your family.

Well, in the thick of my preoccupation with earning more, I got an ironic slap in the face while reading, of all things, *Think and Grow Rich*. I came across a story in which Napoleon Hill suggests to his son that he'd rather him take a job earning 20% less if he'd be learning skills that lead ultimately to workplace success. The latter, he explained, was priceless.

Of course, this was a tough pill for the son to swallow—after all, what's the purpose of a job, if not to earn money? But Napoleon didn't see it that way. You work for all of the resources you gain that teach you how to earn money—the skills, the connections, all the intangibles

Ouch. I was the son. And that didn't change the fact that I was broke. Nevertheless, it was painfully obvious at that moment that I wasn't seeing the big picture.

By narrowing my focus to the pain of not having money, I'd completely neglected the other side of the coin: this job offered me an unprecedented opportunity to "play entrepreneur"—mentorship from global leaders, personal growth, a masters-level education in entrepreneurship. These were all skills I'd someday need to become a real one. As I sulked like a kid upset about tidying up the room paid for by his parents, I neglected to consider the personal growth I still needed to achieve my dream income.

Flip the Coin

Imagine a coin, let's say a quarter. Now, imagine you're holding that quarter in the palm of your hand, heads up, and someone else holds another quarter in theirs, tails up.

If both of you were to describe their view of the quarter to someone who has never seen one before, that person would think you're talking about two different objects. And though both hold the same thing, each description would be partially right and yet ultimately wrong because neither told the whole story.

This is why it's critically important that you evaluate judgments of present reality with a degree of skepticism. There is another side to the story like there's another side to every coin. In the present, we don't have the luxury of hindsight. We don't know how this part will play into the whole of our lives. So I ask, "Is your present the same as your fate? Is what you believe about your future absolute and true? Is it guaranteed to happen?"

I ask you these questions not to undermine your perspective. Your experience of the present matters, just as each chapter plays its role in the arc of a story. Still, sometimes the meanings we assign to the adversity of the present simply reflect an incomplete version of the story that can be.

It's amazing how hard we'll argue that we're fucked and that there's no point in trying to unfuck ourselves. When I ask my coaching clients, "Is it true that's going to happen?" some will insist that the answer is yes. Usually, though, when we dig deeper to assess the certainty of their predictions, the answer turns out to be no.

So the question becomes, "How sure are you?" Of course, no one knows, but they'll insist, "It could happen." Well, yes, anything *could* happen.

To escape the hypotheticals, we need to focus on the one question that matters, here and now—the only question that will impact the future: "Is it beneficial?"

Is it beneficial to focus on the doom-and-gloom version of the part of your story that hasn't been written yet? Because when it comes to the future, no matter how you spin it, it's *all* a fairy tale.

A lot of would-be fairy tales are told as nightmares. We focus on the worst case scenario despite how unlikely those scenarios actually turn out to be. In fact, a recent study showed that less than one in ten of the things people worry about actually happen, and even the ones that do are not as bad as the person imagined they would be. In other words, we waste loads of energy worrying about statistically unlikely things.

"But what if..?" Fuck "what if." Just because some version of the future "might" be true doesn't make it beneficial to entertain. And I don't just mean beneficial from an emotional standpoint. What it also does is place our focus squarely on the negative. So I ask you, how is that beneficial? It's like leading in a race then looking back to see who was gaining on you and tripping over your own two feet. What was the point?

So I say, "Flip the coin." The side of the coin that too many focus on is the one that depicts the nightmare, the hell between your ears that damn near every time turns out worse than the reality. We get so mesmerized by the worst-case scenario that we fail to recognize the fairy tale on the other side of the coin.

A Dead End

Let's pretend for a moment that I have accurate data assuring me with 100% certainty that I'll be dead in five days. I'll be hit by a bus. Or maybe I'll be walking to the bus when an airplane engine randomly lands on my head.

Airplanes fly above us and have engines that could separate from the body and plummet towards one's head—because of gravity. *It could happen.* If I spend my last five days ruminating on my pending death while life happens around me, have I actually lived? In other words, didn't I stop living five days before I actually died?

What if I had flipped the coin and considered all I had to live for, all the gifts in my midst—every relationship, every sunset, every struggle overcome? It's the same coin. Both end with me dead in five days and one hell of a news story. Which one is the more pleasant experience, the guy gazing in awe at the sunset when the engine ends his moment of bliss or the dude scanning the sky for a falling airplane engine and completely missing the epic backdrop?

> The future is a fairy tale.

The future is a fairy tale.

It doesn't exist. All we have is our present. The past and future exist in our heads, memories of what was and projections of what might be—biased ones at that. If we're not careful, they'll distort our experience of the present.

I'm not talking about ignoring reality. I am fully aware that all kinds of horrible fates could come to pass tomorrow. When I flip the coin, I'm not denying the possibility of an outcome I wouldn't have chosen. I love what is and envisioning what wonderful fate could come.

Remember that generally speaking, we are shitty fortune tellers. Not only that, but we're big time Debbie Downers. So when my brain tries to accompany me to the shitshow, I decline and turn it into a hit show. I find it beneficial to be the most Polyanna fucking Nostradamus I can be. The way I see it, if I'm going to be a shitty psychic, I might as well guess on the right side of wrong.

Besides, statistically speaking, I can't do much worse by assuming the positive than most do when they assume the negative. At the very least, I'll have lived life to the fullest by ignoring all of these foreboding predictions that told me to forget about the sunset in case of falling jet engines.

Why? Because I made sure of it. I went through life with the intention of living it to the fullest—seeing all I had and stood to gain, instead of how little I had and all I might lose. Even if it turns out I was full of shit, at least I wasn't passively allowing this bummer of a story to dictate my outlook. At least I could keep moving forward like a pig about to roll around in mud instead of one going to the slaughter.

The Other Side of the Coin

Back in Nashville, I started off as an event producer for the financial education company. In retrospect, the celebrity culture I was operating in, and the access to these great business minds and giants in the industry, justified me earning less than a living wage. And the management had a point—people were paying upwards of ten thousand dollars to hear the secrets of top entrepreneurs in the world. Yes, I was making less than forty grand. And at the same time, I got one step above VIP passes to every event because I was running the show. If I were Napoleon Hill's son, he would've told me to stop whining like a little bitch about the money and get to work.

That said, it'd be hard to argue that I was being paid enough to support a family of four. Which leads to the follow-up question: "Is it beneficial to focus on that?" The answer to that one is now obvious. No. No, it's not. All it was doing was bringing up feelings of helplessness, bitterness, and misery. It was blinding me to all the good this crash course, behind-the-scenes education would eventually do for me. I wonder how much richer that education could've been if I hadn't been too stubborn to embrace it.

Well, eventually I did wake up to the realization that I was getting nowhere focusing on the same busted side of the coin. But I did it with a begrudging attitude. I was watching an interview with Seth Godin where he offered some pretty obvious advice: *If you're not happy with your life, change it.* How's that for tough love? He talked about the principle of *shipping*, deciding your course, and committing to a date by which you'll take decisive action.

> If you're not happy with your life, change it.

By that time, the writing that had been on the wall was circled, underlined, and highlighted enough for me to see—despite the riches of on-the-job education I was getting there, I was still hitting a brick wall when it came to compensation.

So I finally asked myself some tough questions. *Am I going to quit?* No, it wasn't in my nature to throw in the towel then any more than it is today. So it was time to face the music. *Okay, if I'm not going to quit, then how can I deal constructively with this impasse?* In other words, I wondered how I could stop licking my wounds and flip the damn coin.

> I would go to school if, and only if, it served me in a meaningful way.

Well, there's something about flipping the coin that makes seemingly impossible dilemmas much clearer and less painful. I was and remain an opponent of many of the values that higher education stands for. Granted, part of my distaste stems from the fact that I had been denied so many sales jobs solely because I lacked a degree. So I had a chip on my shoulder and still do. It's my "Fuck you, I'll do it without you" mentality. There were legit reasons I had not played into what I saw as a Great American Scam—*give us all your money, bury yourself in debt, and we'll give you a piece of paper proving that you endured an education of questionable value for fake credibility.* And so I promised myself early on that I would *never* go to school to get a piece of paper. I would go to school if, and only if, it served me in a meaningful way.

With my bitterness about lack of pay growing, alongside the goose egg on my head from beating it against that same wall, I flipped the coin. Suddenly, I saw another route that I'd passed up for the entirety of my time at the financial company. *They* would pay for me to earn that piece of paper. For better or worse, a degree was the most glaring difference between me and the coworkers strolling past me like TSA PreCheckers on the security line.

So after years of playing the victim and feeling taken advantage of, I set a date for when I would go back to school. I'd go back on *my* terms and squeeze every freaking ounce of blood I could get out of that turnip. I'd do it for *me*, come away with a degree in my hand and my pride intact. My company would contribute the funding, I'd give the blood, sweat, and tears, and I'd come away with insights and skills that would serve me for life and add to my immediate value as an employee.

Was I scared? Absolutely.

When the date arrived, I had researched colleges, decided on a track, and was enrolled to start less than 30 days later. Was I scared? Absolutely. And yet, I felt at peace. When that date came, I shipped the motherfucker. To that point, all my focus had been on being poor, on not making enough money. Except now, I was going back to school to get a business degree while continuing the all-expenses-paid, on-the-job education that every Master's student wishes they had.

That was the turning point of a journey that had been a continuous struggle for me. And yes, 90% of which was self-imposed, a product of telling myself the same miserable, irredeemable story over and over and over again.

Getting Real

If I flip the coin on that angst-ridden season, I see that it kicked my ass out of lukewarm mediocrity, like being dropped into the ice water of reality. It jolted me out of sleepwalking from dead-end job to dead-end job while thinking, "This time will be different."

Let me give you a little business lesson from the school of hard knocks, where your degree comes in the form of an ego beaten into submission. People aren't going to hand you six figures out of the kindness of their hearts. However, become someone who delivers $1 million plus in value and you can bet your ass they'll lay down the money necessary to keep you around. That's where you've got to start and end—with delivering value that makes you indispensable.

Fuck the carrot. Don't chase anything, especially not something being dangled in front of your face to keep you running.

You have to flip the script from working-to-get to working-to-give. Yes, give for the sake of others. And also, give for *your* sake. Think about it. What puts you in a more powerful position: ruminating on when you might get something or acting upon what you can give? And if everyone's sitting around waiting for someone to give them something, then who's doing the giving? Nobody.

So then, how do you stand out? By flipping the script. Figure out the areas in which you can uniquely add value to that business and the world, the gifts you can offer as no one else can—we've all got 'em.

And that brings us to lesson two from the school of hard knocks: don't go into a job with the audacity of thinking you'll be the one to break through the iron pay ceiling. Not all professions reward effort equally—some require the same or greater effort for dramatically less pay. Want to be rich? Well, I hate to say it, but don't work in the ministry. Don't work in the cage at Marshall's. Not because

> You have to flip the script from working-to-get to working-to-give.

those aren't noble professions. But because you want to be rich, and that's not how your nobility will be repaid in those fields.

If you want to do the good work of helping people *and* drive a Bentley, then you must find a path that allows you to provide immense value to the world. Seek a field where your exceptional contributions are met with equally extraordinary rewards.

Let's imagine that two people with the same elite-level coaching skills take divergent career paths. One decides to go into middle management at a stuffy corporation, the other becomes a business coach. Which is more likely to earn a million dollars in one year? Pretty obvious, right?

I do some coaching ("some" being the operative word). I'm not working anywhere near forty-plus hours a week. And I make a lot more than your average manager. Is that disparity fair? That's not the point. Unless you're going to become an activist and work to overthrow the corporation's compensation structure, you might as well learn to accept what is.

> There was another side to that coin.

The alternative is to become a cog-in-the-machine manager and either squash your high six-figure dreams or bust your ass trying to break through that iron ceiling. Choose the latter, and odds are you're going to end up disappointed and bitter.

Delivering Value

Though I couldn't see at the time, I wasn't honest with myself about where I was in my growth journey. For the first couple of years of work at the financial firm, I was thinking with the mind of an employee and acting with an attitude of entitlement. I wasn't focused on planting seeds for a future harvest. These fuckers had plenty of fruit lying around, and I wanted to eat until I couldn't button my pants. Only then would I consider helping them harvest some more.

Well, guess what? There was another side to that coin, too. The people who started this company and, in particular, the man in charge had started the company when their bellies were rumbling and there wasn't any fruit in sight. The risk was high and the reward was non-existent. They became giants by adding value, not waiting on someone else's harvest. They built the foundation I was standing on, and I wanted the ripest fruits *now*. Looking back, I had it all wrong.

So, after I decided to stay the course and invest in my education, I started asking myself how I might stand out. When I did, I began to notice that people wanted the man on top to speak *all the time*. But it wasn't a priority for him, even if he could have squeezed it into his busy schedule.

The refusals were about more than money or time—I once saw him decline a six-figure offer plus a chartered private jet across the country to speak and be back by lunchtime. It took him less than three seconds to pass because that wasn't the game he was playing. His value was not as a soldier in the field—he was the general back at the Pentagon. He was drawing up the mission and delivering the marching orders that kept projects moving forward.

Hearing him say no stuck with me and sparked a realization of how I could contribute. While the general might not take on the mission of spreading his message through public speaking, there was a way to amplify his voice. By establishing a speaker's bureau, the soldiers could deliver the message for him.

So where before I might have balked at the extra work, now I flipped the coin and started planting the seeds for fruit I'd seen a demand for. Soon I'd written up a proposal and pitched it to the executive vice president.

Within a year, the soldiers were on the ground executing the exact mission I'd proposed. Eventually, I took the helm and grew the venture into a revenue stream exceeding a million dollars, with my income reflecting the value I'd added.

The lesson Napoleon Hill taught his son had reached full fruition in me. This wisdom was far more valuable than any I could've gotten from a stack of money. I'd discovered that I had a gift for starting a business.

I consulted with thousands of companies, identifying their needs and offering practical steps for growth. I found people whose gifts would allow them to fulfill their goals and brainstormed with speakers on how to help companies who were struggling.

> *We make the good more likely when we expect it and get to work making it so.*

Finally, the other side of the coin was in clear view. I began to grasp what it meant to provide a contribution so significant that it couldn't be ignored or left financially unrewarded. Luckily, it wasn't until I got this, my most invaluable on-the-job training, that I realized it was time to move on and level up. But that story will have to wait until the next chapter!

The Flip Side of Challenge

There's no sugarcoating it: no matter what we do and no matter how many factors we leverage in our favor, the cards rarely fall as we'd like them to. At the same time, we're very creative in coming up with all the awful shit that might happen, even though things rarely turn out as bad as the tragic tales we dream up. Remember, we have an active role to play, and we make the good more likely when we expect it and get to work making it so.

MAKING LIFE DOPE:

Let's think about some area of your life that is causing you apprehension. Get out your Life Is Dope journal or workbook and answer these questions:

- What negative life outcome am I focusing on right now?
- Is it true? In other words, is this outcome a definite reality, or merely a magnification of one of many outcomes?
    - Hint: look for where you use the words "fear" and "stress" to zero in on this.
- Is it beneficial?
    - That is, how is focusing on that negative outcome serving you?
- If it's not an absolute certainty, then what else could be possible?
    - What could you start to make possible?

After you answer these questions, take a step back and really analyze what's at play. We often let our thoughts go on autopilot, especially when it comes to worries and fears about the future. But once you start scrutinizing these thoughts—once you put them under a microscope—you might be surprised to find that a lot of them don't hold up.

The point here isn't to sugarcoat reality or ignore challenges. Instead, the aim is to align your focus and energy with what's beneficial and actionable. Don't underestimate the power of a positive outlook. Don't sleep on the faith in your own power to create a better reality.

It's not just a mood booster. Optimism can become a self-fulfilling prophecy. When you expect good things to happen, you act in ways that make those good things more likely.

So, the next time you find yourself spiraling into a doom-and-gloom mindset, flip the coin. Hit pause and run through these questions. It might just be the reality check you need to step back into your power.

BONUS:

What are you waiting for? Dive deeper by using the official Life Is Dope Accompaniment workbook, music playlists and more for absolutely free, by visiting MichaelAnthonyTV.com/LifeIsDope or scanning this QR code:

STORY 6

Fill Your Space

I'll be the king of me
Build on nickels, rubbin' dimes
I'ma turn it to so much more
Chainsmokers, "Kanye"

Let's rewind back to a chapter in my life that predates the trials and tribulations chronicled in the recent pages, a time when my professional journey was taking its first shaky steps.

After I had done my time serving Minneapolis' suburban moms at Marshalls, I saw an opportunity across the mall to help dads fill their emotional gas tanks at the Sears Lawn and Garden department. It was just across the mall and wasn't a step up, per se, but the shift to 100% commissions opened the door for me to raise the ceiling on my earnings. Between all the two-cycle engine oil I planned to sell and the cool twenty G's a year my new bride Sarah was bringing in from her job at a nonprofit, I was sure we'd end up straight ballin'.

> The inmates were running the asylum.

It wasn't long before I realized that the Lawn and Garden department wasn't the center of the action. The dudes who were making bank were across the aisle in the electronics department. And these weren't buttoned-up company men. In the electronics section, the inmates were running the asylum. They were a bunch of savages pumped to the gills with testosterone and ready to sell out their mama for the commissions on a TV. Between the money to be made and the fact that I knew tech from my work with studio gear, I saw an opportunity to level up.

I'm not sure what it says about me, but I felt perfectly at home among the savages. Every one of us was hustling to outdo the others, but with plenty to go around, there were no losers. I was on pace to bring in about forty-thousand dollars in 1999 money, working less than full-time. And I'm here to tell you, you'll never feel as rich on forty grand as you do at twenty. I had time to do my sound gigs, and I was earning a living I was proud of.

And then the new boss showed up.

"Hey, help me push this." Those were his first words to me when I passed him pushing a refrigerator from appliances to electronics before the store had opened. No "Hello." No "What's your name?" Nothing. The dude rubbed me the wrong way right from the jump.

Clearly, nobody had told him that he was signing up as zookeeper to a bunch of wild animals who disregarded all but the laws of the jungle. Why? Because it worked for us. Sales were through the roof, and we were having a ball.

I'd grown accustomed to the hustle of working for commissions, and my take-home pay was growing alongside my skills as a salesman. Since the shift from lawn and garden, I'd gone from bringing home the bacon to serving up a whole breakfast platter. So, I wasn't about to let this guy come in here and tell me where I could eat and shit. And despite my upward

> My take-home pay was growing alongside my skills as a salesman.

trajectory, I decided just like that—*Fuck this, as soon as I can find another job, I'm out.*

From the Sales Floor to the Sales Lot

So what could I do next? Sell some freaking cars, that's what I could do. Within a couple of days, I had landed an interview and was walking into a dealership like I owned the place. And they were eating it up from the get-go—it seemed like a foregone conclusion I was going to get the job. Until they threw me a curveball.

"Are you married?" I wasn't sure what that had to do with anything, but I confirmed nevertheless: "Yes, sir." Well, as soon as the words had left my mouth, the faces of both interviewers dropped and they gave each other a knowing glance. The GM turned back towards me, took a deep breath, and said in a matter-of-fact tone, "I'm not hiring you."

What the hell?

"I'm on my seventh marriage—well, soon to be," he said. "I just divorced wife number six and am about to enter into my seventh marriage." Then he motioned to the assistant GM. "He's on number three. I'm not going to do that to a good kid like you."

I wasn't trying to hear that, though. I had an ego to uphold, and I wasn't going to let a couple of old farts' failed marriages deter me from getting my way. So I crossed those suckers off the list and found another dealership to bless with my presence.

Don't leave yet—fill your space.

This time, the interview was a little more official. They gave me a tour of the place. They interviewed me. They even gave me some kind of personality test to see if I was fit for the job. Then I went on my way and waited for the call.

A few days later at Sears—where I was going through the motions until my backup plan fell into place—there was a phone call for me. On the line was the lady who'd interviewed me at the dealership. "I have some good news for you!" she said. I immediately got a knot in my stomach. In the days since that interview, my ego had shut the fuck up long enough for my conscience to have a say in the matter. Whether it was divine intervention or intuition, the message was clear: *Don't leave yet—fill your space.*

The new boss had bruised my ego, and I was stomping away like a toddler who'd had his toy taken away. *Fine, I'll go play somewhere else!* But it wasn't time to leave my job at Sears. I wasn't leaving from a position of strength and conviction. I was looking for an escape, to relieve pressure. And most importantly, I hadn't yet filled my space. In other words, I wasn't done growing. I was about to dig up the roots that were just becoming established.

"Hello? Are you there?" These revelations hit me like a load of bricks. Three days before, I'd sold myself as though working at this dealership was my dream job, and now I felt like a complete bullshitter. So when I finally responded, all I could come up with was the truth. "I was afraid this was going to happen," I said. "I'm sorry, I have to decline."

Feeling the Heat

I realized I would have to humble myself if I was going to stay in this job. I liked this job. I wanted this job. And it was on me to find a way to coexist with my new boss.

This put a mirror in front of me. I'd let my animosity get in the way of seeing things through his eyes. While my buddy Phil and I were running around using socks and bags as puppets to close deals (100% true story) this poor guy—I found out his name was Dan—was having to toe the line as a company man. And because Sears was struggling and in the middle of a restructure at the time, corporate *stayed* on his ass.

Meanwhile, he was working longer hours than us for a salary that came out to less than ours. In other words, the zookeeper was getting shit on while the wild animals had all the fun.

I could see that Dan was in a thankless position, so I started looking for opportunities to make his life easier. It felt good to help the guy out, and it was obvious that he recognized and appreciated that I had his back. It wasn't long before we became friends, and after a couple of months, he even found an opportunity to help me out. "There's a position coming open in washers and dryers. I think you'd be great over there, and I guarantee you it'll be more money."

He was right. At that time, Sears had all the top-rated models in the industry, and they were flying off the shelves. So from the day I started there and through the next couple of years, I was riding the gravy train with biscuit wheels. Out of nowhere, at twenty-one and with no degree, I'd gone from working full-time for near minimum wage at Marshalls to making fifty-thousand dollars and working no more than thirty-five hours a week.

> I didn't escape. I leaped from a position of strength.

The rest of my time there was pretty damn satisfying. They appreciated me, and I appreciated them. It stayed that way until I saw an opportunity I couldn't pass up: an opening at the Christian music club running live sound—the same club where my friends and I were headed the night that bullets rained down on us.

I wasn't escaping from the job like I'd planned to do a few years prior, but leaping to something full of promise. Something that did, in fact, bloom to more than I had anticipated. As you learned in chapter one, the job wasn't without its own set of problems, and the pay left something to be desired. Nevertheless, during my time there, I went from running live sound to running concert promotions. Then, the club expanded and moved right into the heart of Minneapolis. And once again, life was good.

And why did all that happen? Because I didn't look toward what was next until I had fully filled my space. I didn't escape. I leaped from a position of strength. A few years prior, I had almost walked out with middle fingers and expletives. But because I stayed, I left with hugs and well wishes.

Looking Again to Escape

Nearly a decade later, I found myself in a similar position. My decision to go forward with pursuing the degree I'd scoffed at for so many years turned out to be a mixed bag. On the one hand, it gave me a renewed sense of direction and optimism about the opportunities it might unlock. On the other, my schedule was jam fucking packed. Meanwhile, Sarah had jumped into the insurance industry, and her grass was looking awfully green from where I was sitting.

And where was that? In my bed with a textbook in my hand, a few credits and six months away from dotting the last "I" and crossing the last "T" necessary to get that piece of paper. On top of that, I continued to run the speaker's bureau while *still* waiting to reap the financial benefits of what I had started. The next season of life was so close I could taste it.

It was like the drawn-out end to a Minneapolis winter when you want nothing more than to smell the tulips of spring. All I could do was get through each day, exhausted from the constant effort of growing myself, and the speaker's bureau, with seemingly little return. Finally, I decided starting something new was the answer. Instead of changing myself, I'd force a change of seasons.

Yes, I was ignoring signs that the grass only looked greener on Sarah's side because it seemed so fucking brown on mine. At the time, she was working for some shady characters. These were guys who lied so much you wondered if they remembered what the truth was.

> *My attitude was all wrong.*

Even with the chance to launch a new speaker's bureau funded by the company, and despite having access to world-class mentorship that amounted to the ultimate paid internship, I still hadn't shaken the counterproductive belief that I was getting screwed over.

My attitude was all wrong. Yes, I had been paying my dues. And yes, my pay had been modest at best. At the same time, the hard work of getting the speaker's bureau off the ground was done. Instead of reaping all the seeds I'd sown, I was planning my escape. My mind was saying something that should have sounded pretty familiar—*Fuck this, as soon as I can find another job, I'm out.*

A Lesson From the Past

Was I being paid less because of the comp I'd started with? Sure. Had I finished the job I'd started? Nope. When I took the initiative to start the speaker's bureau, I was stepping out in faith. I was going from being a hub in the wheel to building a new one. Now, I had the opportunity to prove myself faithful—to the company, yes, but even more so to myself. I had seen a space to be filled, but I had not yet filled it.

Now, a decade older and a bit wiser, I looked back on that kid who ignored the ego that was demanding, "I want to go NOW!" Instead, he had listened to the conscience who was answering, "When it's time, you'll know." I also reflected on the way I left Sears—if I'd quit earlier, I would've carried bitterness and a preoccupation with how I "deserved" to be treated, which would've tainted the next season of my life.

> I was mistaking my vision of who I could be, with where I actually was.

In retrospect, I was mistaking my vision of who I could be, with where I actually was. In my mind, I was a person deserving of the fruits of my labor. Except I was missing a step. Yes, I was deserving of the fruits, and I had to finish the job that ensured I got them. I had not reached that potential and filled that space. And I still wanted to quit. The winter was dragging on, the buds were struggling to break through, and I was about to walk away.

I wouldn't leave with so much unfinished business and unresolved feelings. So in spite of my impatience to cross into insurance, I stayed and saw the company I had started through. I even redoubled my efforts as the reach of the company continued to expand.

And what was the end result? That operation reached a point when it was off the ground and running, bringing in more than $1 million in revenue. And I was promoted to a vice president level of the operation, which included the salary that had forever seemed out of my reach.

And, that's when it was time to leave. Ironic, right? I had filled my space. Did it hurt getting there? Yes. And despite the objections of my ego, I stuck it out even as my dream timeline dragged out.

While things were going along well, Sarah made a move from the insurance company run by crooks to a company truly about helping people. With that move came an opportunity for me to join her. We could see that this was a chance to transform our lives and the lives of others. And that's exactly what we did and have done since.

Looking back, I learned 90% of the most valuable lessons in the last 10% of my time at the Speaker's Bureau—the time I came closest to missing out on. Not only that, but I was proud of what I had accomplished. I left in a place of strength, knowing that, finally, I had filled my space.

Embracing Growth Through Tension

The paradox of the dope life is this: it doesn't always look pretty. True growth, the kind that fills our space and leads to deep fulfillment, often comes dressed in the guise of pressure and discomfort. We don't ascend to the next level without facing and passing the tests laid out before us. Each test passed grants us the grace to endure greater tension, opening the door to more transcendence and growth.

The cost of doing what we want often means doing what we don't. To truly fill the space you're in and rise to the occasion of great opportunities, you'll be given the gift of confronting discomfort or completing tasks that feel mind-numbing. I'm where I'm at today because I disciplined myself to find joy in the fact that the inconvenient, painful things represent the key to success in life. So as much as we'd like to skip to the good part and leave for the "greener grass," like I almost did, that's not how the dope life works.

There's no one who has excelled in life who didn't struggle along the way. Does that mean they enjoyed it? Hell no! It's simply a matter of vision—they saw that the road to where they wanted to be passed through difficulty, not around it. And they accepted that. They recognized tension as their friend, the usher to growth, and that allowed them to meet it with grace.

> There's no one who has excelled in life who didn't struggle along the way.

MAKING LIFE DOPE:

Now, I want you to grab your Life Is Dope journal or workbook and think about this:

- What would it feel like to embrace tension and discomfort as not just inevitable but beneficial? Remember, they are the hallmarks of growth, the price of admission to the life you desire.
    - How can you start seeing these discomforts as your allies rather than your enemies?
- What would it look like to find joy in the inconvenient or painful tasks?
    - How can you re-frame them as essential steps toward your larger goals?
    - What tasks have you been avoiding that might actually be stepping stones to success?
- What if you redefined your perspective on struggle and success? What if it's not about avoiding challenges but embracing them as part of the journey?
    - Choose one challenge you've been calling "struggle." As you write, how can you change your perspective and see it as a sign that you're on a beneficial path?
- Consider your contributions and growth in your current role or situation.
    - Are you planting seeds in the soil you're standing on, or are you always looking for the next field?
    - How is this helping or hurting you?
    - How can you make the most of where you are now?

You see, pain ain't no thing to a giant. The pressure squeezes the shit out of us, and in the end, we're a more refined version of ourselves. It transforms suffering into a catalyst for growth, teaching us to redefine our battles, not as insurmountable obstacles but as opportunities to rise above, to expand beyond the confines of our former selves.

> *Reaching the next level comes as a result of the character-building part.*

Thank God for tension. Were the roads always clear, the skies blue, and the wind at our backs, we'd fail to appreciate the victories won through grit and ingenuity. Reaching the next level comes as a result of the character-building part. I can see clearly now that not a single step could've been skipped to get me where I am today. And that the growth in each season of my life made me who I am today. The net result is I am a changed and changing man.

The same can be true for you, as well. Who knows what the next season will hold when you've fully filled the space of this one?

BONUS:

Dive deeper by using the official Life Is Dope Accompaniment workbook, music playlists and more for free, by visiting MichaelAnthonyTV.com/LifeIsDope or scanning this QR code:

STORY 7

Know The Game You're Playing

Life's about film stars and less about mothers
It's all about fast cars and cussing each other
But it doesn't matter 'cause I'm packing plastic
And that's what makes my life so fuckin' fantastic
—**Lily Allen, "The Fear"**

The successful establishment of the speaker's bureau at the financial education organization marked a turning point, presenting two distinct paths for my professional future. Either I was going to continue fighting my way up the corporate ladder—to more money, more prestige, and more obligations—or I was going to find my way as an entrepreneur. As you learned in the last chapter, I soon realized I was ready for option two.

> The more successful I became as an employee,
> the more empty I felt inside.

For my first couple of decades as a professional, I'd chosen option one. Truth be told, I wasn't yet at the point in my life where I was ready to go it alone. In those years, I needed a path laid out for me.

Except there was a problem with that route—the more successful I became as an employee, the more empty I felt inside.

Three factors were driving my discontent. First, I was grappling with a lifetime of hurt and trauma that needed tending to. And I was losing. I still had work to do on myself, work that required time, money, and commitment. Well, after years of barely scraping by, I finally had the money. My time and commitment, though, were stretched as thin as they'd ever been.

The second problem was that I deeply desired a more consistent home life, one where I could come home every night and help my kids with their homework, cook them dinner, and put them to bed. I was traveling non-stop, and my kids were more grown up each time I came home. And as they got older, I was less and less involved in raising them—I was a company man, toeing every line and going every extra mile. The payoff, though, wasn't in the work itself.

And that was the third and overarching factor: I dreamed of blazing a path of my own, one driven by fulfilling my own purposes, not someone else's. At the same time, Sarah was finding meaning not only as a mother but also as a professional. She was working to get her own insurance agency off the ground and that inspired me. Sarah was living out her purpose, one I believed in wholeheartedly and knew that I could contribute to with my abilities.

I knew I wanted more out of life. I knew I wanted a life I didn't need a vacation from. And now it was time to intentionally design it.

So I left.

I had filled my space at the financial education organization. I'd gotten my feet wet as an entrepreneur through the speaker's bureau and made my long-coveted six figures. Now it was time to step into the insurance agency, to come team up with Sarah as a co-owner where we could build it to something bigger and better together.

My responsibility was to expand the agency. I'd be seeking out agents who, like Sarah, were in search of a flexible schedule while earning as much as they wished. In many ways, it felt preordained. The role put me in the position to grant others what I had desired for so long—the chance to design whatever the dope life looked like for them. Ironically, I'd left the nine-to-five life just as I'd reached my long-coveted six-figure income. Because I had found my deeper why.

The Game of (Your) Life

Life is a collection of categories, each requiring a degree of commitment that ultimately adds up to the game you're playing. For example, you can give damn near 100% of your time and energy to your career and skip turn after turn playing father, mother, spouse, or friend. If your primary identity is that of a businessperson, excellence in other areas may elude you, not due to lack of interest but because they aren't your central focus.

For every aspect of life and each game you play, there are rules—some imposed, others self-assigned. In a business setting, you can't show up at noon when you're scheduled at nine. Why? Because you'll be fired—break the rules enough times, and your disqualification from the game is inevitable.

If you are the boss and consistently show up at noon when you know it's in the best interest of the business for you to arrive at nine, well, you might not be "dismissed" from the game, but the game itself will eventually unravel and your business will fail.

I had found my deeper why.

The same goes for family life. If you skip dinner time too often, don't be shocked if things feel off at home. It's like jumping into a game late and wondering why you're not in sync with everyone else.

Whether self-determined or imposed, we have the choice of whether to follow the rules. Just remember that ignoring them, whether intentionally or not, often leads to chaos.

Most people don't take the time to contemplate how the games they choose to play define their lives. They never pause and consider whether the rules they abide by are beneficial or detrimental. They live by obligation, never questioning if their actions align with their best interests.

Other people object loudly about their life's direction with no real intention of acting to change it. They go on and on about circumstances beyond their control and bemoan situations they willingly entered—the job they don't intend to leave, the HOA rules they signed up for when they moved in, the debt that they accrued through their own choices. Ultimately, their tantrum comes from participating in a game that doesn't align with their desires. While at the same time, they continue to adhere to its rules. Rather than take steps to effect change, they direct all their dissatisfaction and irritation toward the very circumstances they've chosen.

What they all have in common is they play a game they don't like by rules they never think to question. *Is this who I truly am? Does this serve me? Are my present priorities heading in the direction of the person I want to be?*

All that begs the question: how can a person achieve success without intention? If I were to ask ten people to tell me why they chose their career, nine out of ten wouldn't be able to answer me with any real conviction. They're going through the motions—doing what their dad did, what seemed like fun, what brings in money. In each case, their alleged purpose falls short of answering the question, *why?* Why do you want more money? *Well, I want a nice life.* Deeper—why do you want a nice life? *Well, it's better than the alternative.* Why is that better than the alternative?

Asking *why* brings clarity. Clarity leads to decisive action. Decisive action brings about meaningful change—meaningful because it's driven by purpose. That's the upward cycle of success, and that's where we find fulfillment—through living out the answer to our *why*.

Run Your Race

The "summer from hell," as Sarah and I now refer to it, began in the spring and extended into fall, just after we established our business. I can't begin to tell you how many times we "quit" during this time. All I know is that it happened multiple times a day, though luckily we never both threw in the towel at the same time

That summer, I didn't understand the game I'd signed up for. No instruction booklet laid out the rules. There was no clear indication of how to win. I did, however, manage to identify my competitors.

But before I tell you about that, let me preface it with this: comparison is a bitch—especially if you are as competitive as me. Why? Because when your life is built upon comparison, you're trying to be faster, stronger, do more, and earn more than *all* the others. That either assigns you to the role of winner or loser, and neither is particularly helpful to keep you focused on the game you're playing—*your* game.

> Comparison is a bitch.

When we began our insurance agency I had certain ideas of success in mind, and they were based almost entirely on the example of others in the same field. From very early on, I started comparing our numbers to businesses that were achieving superior results and more rapid expansion.

At the same time, I ignored businesses with similar or inferior performance levels, much less those who, like us, had launched much later than the seasoned companies I obsessively tracked. In other words, I was only looking at narrow aspects of business when making comparisons. Sure, we were just getting started, but I wanted success *now*. Do you know the feeling?

Lost in all of this were the *whys* that motivated my transition into entrepreneurship in the first place. I had three purposes, and none had to do with the competition's numbers—I wanted to improve myself, spend more time with my kids, and build a dynasty. And yet somehow, I ended up watching the scorecards my self-assigned competitors used to measure their success.

The problem? Their scorecards didn't even reflect the purposes I'd set out to achieve. I'd forgotten all about the game I'd decided to play and the rules that mattered to me. And by focusing on business at the expense of my deepest purposes, I was unsurprisingly falling short on all three.

I was also miserable company to myself and my family. Even when I was there, I wasn't present. This new game wasn't working, and something had to change.

And so, I recommitted to self-care, dedicating about twenty hours a week to activities like reading, journaling, and therapy. That process of excavating all that I'd been neglecting entailed a lot of pain. I faced many demons and ventured into some dark corners of my soul. Ones that I'd avoided for a reason. Some I'm still working through today.

What I didn't fully realize at the time, though, was that all this demon-wrestling and dark corner dwelling was strengthening me, making me more resilient in the face of struggle. And the more whole I became, the more I could give as a father, partner, and business leader.

> The more whole I became, the more I could give.

Alongside my renewed commitment to personal growth, I made a pivotal shift in how I approached our business. Far from pulling back, I cut out all the fluff that my employee mindset had taught me about looking busy. Instead, I stayed *hyper*-focused on what truly moved the needle.

Most people can give a solid four hours of highly productive work on their best days. Knowing this, I committed to giving four hours a day of intense focus to our business, no more and no less. Every day. This wasn't about doing less, it was about doing more in less time and with greater consistency.

And something ironic happened when I turned my focus away from the numbers of my competitors and toward being the father and human I wanted to be: cooking dinners, helping with homework, and offering my full presence. By returning to my why and re-clarifying my purpose, I unknowingly initiated an upward cycle of success.

This wasn't about being superhuman. It was about being super *consistent. Every. Fucking. Day.* And eventually, thanks to maintaining a commitment to both my personal growth and my business effort, the insurance company worked itself out. To put it plainly, we kicked *ass.*

> This wasn't about being superhuman. It was about being super consistent.

Success on *Your* Terms

The story is far too common and the danger all too real: a person works hard for years on end—maybe for their entire career—only to look back and realize that all of their striving led them farther and farther from who they were. They check the map and their GPS dot is in the middle of a gray zone.

But you don't have to go out like that. As long as you're breathing, you can consult your conscience, recommit to your values, and find your way back.

By reclaiming the game I was playing, I began the process of recovering the self I'd buried under rules that didn't serve me. Since then, I've healed wounds that were once so deep and pain so pervasive that I didn't know life could be any other way. I now feel peace where there was once angst and strength where there was once weakness.

And yes, our business is thriving, but more important than that, it's impacting lives. Take Heather, for example. I watched her use the six-figure-plus income she earned in her first year in a new industry to put her husband through school. Her's is one of hundreds of stories I could tell of people achieving true fulfillment by defining success on their own terms with our company.

Creating Your Own Scorecard

Knowing the game you're playing isn't just about being strategic or outwitting competitors—it's about understanding what truly matters to you and aligning your scorecard to those standards—your standards. You can rack up wins all day long, but if those victories aren't contributing to a life that resonates with your core values, then it's like winning rounds in a game you never wanted to play.

As Simon Sinek so insightfully advised, the key is to "Start with why." Why? Because success unfolds from the inside out—it begins with your relationship with yourself, extends to the dynamics within your home, and then permeates into your professional life. Your why influences your career, business strategies, and interactions with employees and colleagues in the broader public sphere.

> *Your why influences your career, business strategies, and interactions.*

MAKING LIFE DOPE:

So, as we move forward, take out your Life Is Dope journal or workbook and respond to the following:

- Why are you doing what you're doing? Is the game you're playing aligned with what truly matters to you? Reflect on your "why."

- What rules have you been playing by?
  - Hint: look for what brings you great joy (and pain) to find rules in your life.
- Are these rules temporary or lifelong? For example, is it for a short-term season because your kid is three years old?
- What rules are serving you and do you want to keep them?
- What's one rule that's no longer serving you?
- If you could invent the game you're playing, how would you want it played and scored?
- What would have to be true for you to live a life with these rules?

Answering these questions will make sure that the game of life you're playing is one you actually want to win. You'll ensure its rules make sense to you and its prizes truly enrich your life and the lives of those you care about. Only then can you say that you're winning, and winning where it counts.

BONUS:

You know what I'm about to say. Dive deeper by using the official Life Is Dope Accompaniment workbook, music playlists and more for free, by visiting MichaelAnthonyTV.com/LifeIsDope or scanning this QR code. And if you already did this, tag me on social @MichaelAnthonyTV so I can give you a virtual high five!

STORY 8

People Like Us Do Things Like This

> *All I do is win, win, win no matter what*
> *Got money on my mind I can never get enough*
> *And every time I step up in the building*
> *Everybody hands go up!*
> —DJ Khaled, "All I Do Is Win"

In 2008, after we sold our brownstone in Minneapolis, Sarah and the kids were finally able to join me in Nashville. This was during the worst global financial crisis since the Great Depression, a time when millions of people had lost their homes to foreclosure. It also marked the twilight of an era when someone with a low income and a low credit score could borrow money for a home.

> People like them lived like that.

Enter my family.

The factors that made 2008 such a shitshow for many allowed Sarah and I to buy up a foreclosure in a nicer part of town than we ever would have considered. And so, we suddenly found ourselves living among the rich suburbanites whose lifestyle had been completely alien up to that point.

People like *them* lived like *that*.

Except now, here I was—one of "them." At heart, though, I was still the guy who got off work at the Mall of America and drove past the pristine, manicured section of Minneapolis feeling a gnawing sense of judgment. Why? Because I assumed they looked down on me, so it was easier for me to judge them first than to be vulnerable and risk getting hurt.

I spent some time in the suburbs as a kid. During that season, our neighbors reported us to the city because our house was in disarray—uncut grass, cars with broken windows, and flat tires in the driveway. In retrospect, the issue was us. Now, the issue was me.

Driving in my new hood, I felt like a guy who'd showed up at the office without his pants on. That feeling of standing out was never more blatant than the day I dropped my daughter off at the house of a friend from kindergarten. I rolled up in my Nissan Altima, a car I lovingly referred to as Lightning McQueen.

Sure, it wasn't shiny or fast or sexy or anywhere close to new. But it was red—sort of. Each year of sun exposure had peeled away the original paint to reveal some new shade of red beneath the protective finish. This was Lightning McQueen with a Tow Mater paint job. But, I preferred driving a car I was embarrassed by over having a car payment, so Mater McQueen made his way to the 'burbs.

> I preferred driving a car I was embarrassed of over having a car payment.

A little self-deprecating humor was enough to take the sting out of owning a car that mirrored my mindset. It wasn't in good shape. It wasn't very comfortable. It more or less worked to get me from point A to point B, but not very far beyond that. It certainly didn't command anyone's respect, but at least it existed alongside plenty of other cars that would have been long past their heydays if they'd ever had one in the first place.

True, Lightning was a five-hundred-dollar car, but dammit, he was *my* five-hundred-dollar car, and he'd carried me all the way to this pristine, bleached-white driveway, framed by a lawn manicured tighter than Ryan Gosling's jawline.

I prayed as if my life depended on it that I could drop my daughter off before anyone spotted me, but I was a sitting duck. This house was in the neighborhood adjoining ours, where the cars, homes, and residents were even more fancy than the ones on our side of the hood.

So knowing my daughter wasn't yet strong and agile enough to vacate a moving vehicle, I did what any good dad would do—pushed her out of the passenger door with a stiff arm that would've made Adrian Peterson proud.

My timing couldn't have been worse.

As I backed down the driveway, here came the dad, pulling up in a car as impeccably maintained as his hairstyle as he waved and flashed a smile as white as his driveway. Meanwhile, I was a nervous wreck, and my internal dialogue only made things worse—"Holy shit, holy shit, holy shit. People like them live like that. Poor people like me live like this. *He's not like me.*"

> I was terrified of people with money.

But he was looking me square in the eye, seemingly oblivious to my polychrome red paint job. I had no choice but to greet him. So I pulled up and started to roll down the window when I remembered—it's freaking broken and won't go down all the way.

To be fair, race cars typically don't have operable windows, but at that moment, any semblance of humor I'd been able to conjure about my car and the lifestyle it represented was drowned out by the crushing shame of who I was. Or more accurately, who I wasn't.

Even today, my heart rate speeds up and my palms get sweaty thinking about that moment. I was terrified of people with money.

Among the Minions

Flash forward four years later and Sarah had been to a few insurance conferences by now, but this was just my second. By this time, Sarah had moved from the insurance company with questionable leadership to the company that would become "home." I was still at the speaker's bureau, and I'd gotten the license that would bridge my move to the insurance agency.

In the time left over from growing the bureau and being "Mr. Mom" at night, I started to establish what would eventually become my role in our company: recruiting new agents.

While Sarah played the role of power producer, going out and making sure families were protected, I held down the home front. Though we still had a long way to go, we were a damn good team, and for the first time in a while, it felt like we were firing on all cylinders. Momentum was on our side and, all things considered, life was pretty good.

Though this was one of my first conferences, I could see that this one was different from what I was used to. For one, I was excited to attend it. There were no blatant sales pitches, no gimmicks, just a company run by real people.

As someone who'd made a living producing events and consulting with thousands of companies, I'd seen my fair share of "performers," people who were all smiles onstage and all assholes offstage. In this company, though, the warmth displayed to the public was bigger in private. It was a good group.

Nevertheless, I was all but checked out when it came time for the big reveal I'd witnessed the last time I had attended the event. A few of *them*, the star agents at Symmetry Financial Group, would be announced as the qualifiers of an Alaskan Cruise for their standout performances, and then we'd all go home, back to the grind.

Usually, the qualifiers looked something like the dad I met through the crack in my window that day: radiant smile, immaculate hair, well dressed, general air of confidence that said, "I belong here." To be honest, I hated this part. Why? Because people like *them* lived like *that*—and they were not like me. History had proven I was not the type of person who received recognition or earned anything as a result of my efforts.

Yet, deep down, I wanted what they had. At one point, I'd ripped out an ad in a magazine for one of these events and set it next to my bed where I would see it every night. With everything and everyone telling me to give up on my dream, the ad tormented as much as it inspired me.

By all appearances, my doubters had a point. By the time I sat down in that ballroom, I'd given my heart to work in ministry for less than a living wage. I'd been paid the chump change leftover from the stacks of money I made for the printing company. Now, I had just graduated, was establishing the speakers bureau, was on daddy duty several nights a week, and recruiting to our infantile insurance agency, so Sarah could be out there hustling.

> Yet, deep down, I wanted what they had.

I continued to give my all to the bureau despite knowing my heart was no longer in it. Sarah and I were in the trenches together. There was so much hope for us in that season, so much excitement, so much life and togetherness. To just figure it out, no matter the risk or cost. We had decided to go all in.

So on that day, I was pretty exhausted, happy to be there among hopeful energy and great people—and at the same time, about as worn out as the car I was driving. Then, as I waited patiently for the last round of names and applause breaks, the course of events took an astonishing detour, jarring me from my stupor—this time, *we* were one of them.

Taking the Stage

I can still see it today, standing up on that stage, all the lights converging on the 35 or so company MVPs, which, this time, included Sarah and me. It's almost like a dream now, and it wasn't so different at the time—looking out onto a sea of smiling faces, feeling a palpable energy from the crowd I'd been a part of just seconds before. I felt like Jay-Z taking the stage at Madison Square Garden, only there were a few hundred fans rather than twenty thousand. This was a *big* deal to me.

> This was a big deal to me.

There was a moment when I looked towards the back of the auditorium and was struck by the stark contrast between the radiance of the stage and the darkness out there. "That was me," I thought looking across the hundreds of attendees whose efforts remained unseen and unacknowledged—in the dark. "That's where I thought I belonged."

The lead-up was far from sexy, and the road was not smooth. We were running on blind faith, never sure that our work and sacrifice would be rewarded. You hear people say all the time that achieving something monumental doesn't matter. Bullshit. Claiming that big wins don't matter is a delusion to soften the blow when you've laid it all out on the table and come up short. Nothing hurts worse than knowing you've given it your all only to realize it wasn't enough—that you are *not* like them.

> *The "this" that people like "us" do isn't winning awards. That's only the fruit that emerges after all the work.*

And I'd grown so accustomed to losing that I'd all but accepted it as my identity. A *loser.* Leading up to that announcement, I was a lot like my car: worn out and barely running. But after 220,000 miles, Lightning McQueen had kept going, kept plodding ahead in blind faith that somewhere, someday, he'd reach the pearly gates on the other side of hell.

Now on that stage, *I* was the one being celebrated. I had watched people like them do things like this, and now I was one of them? *What?!* How did I get here? Was I really any different now than before I made my way to this stage?

Of course not. The "this" that people like "us" do isn't winning awards. That's only the fruit that emerges after all the work behind the scenes and beneath the surface. The roots have to push their way into the dark recesses of the soil. Only then can the nutrients make their way to the surface, and only then do the fruits and their rewards emerge.

By the time I hit that stage, I had invested 220,000 miles worth of blood, sweat, and tears into pushing my way down through the soil to manifest my rightful self. I had spent years forging ahead on faith alone, saving and investing what minuscule extra money I had to work on myself. More times than I can count, I watched people around me succeed and felt like an imposter by comparison.

And yet, even when doubt crept in, I kept going. Even when family members who loved me questioned the value of investing in these events that seemed to lead nowhere, I kept going.

Yes, it was dark beneath the surface. But what they couldn't see—the thing I sometimes questioned and never abandoned—was that this tree was planted on paydirt.

Uncovering Who You've Always Been

We hear so much about the value of personal growth and all the ways of getting stronger, faster, and smarter. But there's another kind of self-improvement, one that gets far less press despite being equally important.

And this kind is necessary if we're to get any real, soul-level benefit from all those efforts to become more than we currently are. When we take root in that thing that lights us up, and we continually nourish it, that's when we become who we are wired to be.

This process isn't about becoming someone new. It's about discovering and accepting who we are and have always been. Me and that car had more in common than years of wear and tear. Once upon a time, that mofo was as red as a vine-ripe chili pepper. He was Lightning motherfucking McQueen.

> *This process isn't about becoming someone new. It's about discovering and accepting who we are and have always been.*

We are the "us" in people like us. The greatness in me is the greatness in you. It's the greatness in every person who will read this book. I belong. You belong. Life is the relentless excavation of that person underneath the muck and the rubble, the magnificent sculpture that remains once we've chipped away the stone to unveil our true selves.

For that to seem worthwhile, though, you have to trust that there's brilliance there. And if you don't, then trust me, a person who was stripped of everything but his faith on the way to expressing the greatness hidden beneath the surface. Your conviction points the way to redemption. Follow it, and sooner or later, your efforts will prove me right.

> *Your conviction points the way to redemption. Follow it.*

They did for me and countless clients I've coached. And while getting the award was the realization of all my dreams and work, it didn't bring about an overnight change of mindset. That's because we never fully arrive. We never reach perfection. And sometimes, our circumstances change before our emotions catch up. Yes, I'd finally pushed my roots deep enough for a tiny bud to emerge, and still, I had more digging to do than I could have imagined.

Nevertheless, winning that award and its accompanying trip changed me. I didn't know it or have the words for it at the time, but later, I encountered the Seth Godin phrase you've heard throughout this chapter that perfectly captured the transformation that moment initiated in me.

People like us do things like this.

Despite overwhelming evidence to the contrary and continued questioning about why I kept driving a ramshackle car and watering a barren tree, I stayed true to my convictions. I did the "things like this" that eventually led to uncovering the person I'd always felt myself to be. As a result, I'd spent years doing "things like this" before I became a person who looked like them.

I stepped out of the bright lights of that stage, my heart pounding with newfound energy and purpose. Yet as I returned to the shadows, ready to resume my relentless pursuit, I couldn't shake the feeling that the man who emerged was not the same one who had entered. I took that stage in August. I took the trip to Alaska in September. And thanks to some sage advice from Gary V, by November 1st, I was ready to go all-in on a new phase of life—I quit my job and joined Sarah full-time. This was the wake-up call I needed. I was worthy. People like us do things like this–we go all in.

Eventually, our roots expanded beyond the capacity of the same grounds that had swallowed them up years earlier. Knowing it was time for us to make the move to a place where we could continue to grow, we considered a home that was enough space to be grateful for, but cheap enough to ensure that we could easily cover the costs and have plenty left over.

> *I was worthy.*

Was it the house of our dreams? No, it wasn't. And did it give us ample room to grow? Again, the answer was no.

There was another house that we could've bought, but it pushed our comfort zone beyond what we were accustomed to. It was a house that aligned with my emerging identity as someone who expects to grow into the future, to have and bless others in abundance.

The path to that growth was not clear, but the choice was. People like *us* buy homes like this. Our decision to buy that house led me to where I sit today, in a home a cut above the one just a few doors down, where years ago a guy in an old beat-up Nissan Altima dropped his daughter off to play.

MAKING LIFE DOPE:

The road of conviction goes through hell. The same road leads to heaven.

At this pivotal moment, I ask you to pause, grab your Life Is Dope journal or workbook, and consider where your own conviction is leading you. It's more than just a path; it's a journey that shapes who you are and who you become.

> *The path to that growth was not clear, but the choice was.*

- Identify your conviction. What is the vision for yourself that you can't shake off, who deep down you believe you are? This is the essence of your drive, the core of your being that pushes you toward your dreams. Write it down.
- Who is your "us"? These are the people, the ideals, and the values that you align with, that make up the fabric of your life.
  - Does your "us" ground you in a set of beliefs that support your growth and your journey?
- Now define your "them." These are individuals you see as different or more accomplished. Contrast their lives with yours, not as a means of diminishing your own worth but as a learning tool.

- Commit to one "people like us". What's one action you could take today to begin laying the roots that will reveal the person buried underneath the muck of life?
    - This step is about turning your vision into reality, one small and significant action at a time.

For me, "us" were the entrepreneurs and the wealthy neighbors whom I perceived to live without stress, a judgment, and self-handicap that only led me to conclude, "Well, I can't do that"—the dreaded four-letter word. Bullshit. I could and so can you. People who are growing do things like this—they take full ownership over their words, thoughts, and actions. What have you observed of "them" that you can learn from?

Bullshit. I could and so can you.

As you move forward, carry these reflections with you. Let them guide your actions and inform your choices. The road of conviction is challenging, and it's also incredibly rewarding. It's your path to becoming the person you've always dreamed of. Because who knows? Maybe they, too, rode into town in a five-hundred-dollar car.

BONUS:

Have you dived deeper yet? Use the official Life Is Dope workbook, music playlists and more for absolutely free, by visiting MichaelAnthonyTV.com/LifeIsDope or scanning this QR code.

STORY 9

The Future Is a Fairy Tale

You can't take it with ya,
and your whip ain't gon' miss ya
So wipe off that window
and see the bigger picture now
—Andy Grammar, "85"

It took another encounter with the merciless reality of death to reawaken me from my stupor.

I had learned this lesson years before, or so I thought. Untimely death was a part of life in the neighborhood of Minneapolis where I grew up. Even then, it took my own brush with death that night in Minneapolis to jolt me from complacency into an understanding of what it means to appreciate the gift of being alive each day.

That night, I woke up to the reality that tomorrow is a fairy tale, and the flesh-and-blood story happens moment by moment.

And yet, despite the prevalence of death in my formative years and brushes with it as a young adult, all thoughts of mortality had gotten lost in the rat race. By my mid-thirties, I was busy, comfortably ignorant, and the reality that each story has an unchosen end had once again receded into the shadows.

Now, that familiar but long-neglected foe overtook me again. Suddenly, there was a real possibility that I would lose not one, not even two, but three of the people most dear to me. Yes, over four months, *three* of my best friends—Tommy, Jodi, and Hugo—got diagnosed with cancer. Then a couple of years later, my super close friend Jimmy got his diagnosis.

Hugo was a guy who went through life with a low-key, no-BS presence concealing a heart of Herculean proportions. He was a proud Hispanic and Texan, a former first responder and fireman, and a man of as few words as close friends. There was no one better to have on your side than Hugo, and it was never lost on me how lucky I was to be called his friend.

One night, we were over at Hugo's house playing some family board games when he mentioned going down to the beach in Pensacola, Florida for fall break. Without a beat, my mind reached for the old, worn-out scarcity script: *Nope, can't afford it. We have a vacation fund with a balance of zero. We've never done this before. Sorry, this is not something "people like us" do.*

But that was none of Hugo's concern. He had just beaten cancer. Yep, Hugo made it. A bunch of our friends were going, including Jodi. If Hugo was my brother-from-another-mother, then Jodi was my sister-from-another-mister, and she, too, had just found out she was cancer-free.

This was going to be a celebration of life among the people who had almost lost theirs. It was also intended as a tribute to Tommy, the third of those diagnosed, and the one who didn't make it.

Hugo wanted us all to be a part of this moment.

And yet, none of that made it past the programming that said, *Danger: spend that money and you will drown!* We'd finally reached a point in life where we were out of the pit of financial despair. I'd reached the holy grail I'd chased for so long, the "if only" that seemed forever out of reach—a six-figure income. We'd paid off our house. The insurance business we'd built piece-by-piece was now beginning to take flight.

In other words, we had the money. I just didn't have any practice with having it. I knew how to be poor—I was damn good at it. I could brave the high seas with the whole family squeezed on a broken ass piece of wood the size of one of those "Blessed" signs they sell at Marshalls. *Buy a raft? Bah, we'll make it through on this.* Unfortunately, that's all I'd learned to focus on. Surviving. And along the way, I had unwittingly adopted a catchphrase: "We can't afford it."

Now, I was clinging to this sliver of wood while my friends waved me onto the party pontoon.

We can't afford it. We can't afford it!

I was so terrified that if we spent our money, I'd end up back in the chaos and poverty I came from. And yet, I might as well have been poor anyway. I was so preoccupied with what I stood to lose by spending money that I was oblivious to all I stood to gain by investing it in what mattered.

And what could matter more than this? Had my friends not made it, I would've been left facing regret with no remedy. Now I had the chance to express all my love to the people who I'd been afraid wouldn't be around to hear it.

> We're going to go make memories that cannot be taken away.

My catchphrase was still playing on repeat, but the moment I caught the look of anticipation on Hugo's face, all of the noisy rationalizations from that old, familiar killjoy fell silent. Against all my instincts and with very little thought, I decided—we're going to go make memories that cannot be taken away.

That decision marked the close of a chapter that had long overstayed its welcome. The trip turned out to be so rich with love and meaning that we continued to gather in celebration of being alive each year for the next decade. The group grew every time—at the peak, we were rolling thirty-five deep. We squeezed more memories into each of those weeks than most do in a year.

The decision to join my friends in Pensacola cost me about fifteen hundred bucks. I could've kept a tight grip on that, and I would have traded those memories for the false promise of "survival" in another day of not really living at all. I would have continued to miss the point that life is meant to be *lived*.

A Selfie to Remember

I am an adamant proponent of selfies. Consequently, I have quite the collection, but one that's most dear to me is of a special gathering we had in honor of Jimmy.

Jimmy grew up with nineteen siblings, which has to be some kind of record, and I'm convinced he never lost a fight with one of them. Jimmy was a scrapper in *everything* he did, and that included loving people and loving life. When necessary, his love was harsh—he took hold of every ounce of joy life had to offer and was willing to put himself into the fire to challenge the people he loved to do the same.

> "I'm not a statistic, suckas."

Nobody walked away from their time with Jimmy without a few crazy stories and a renewed zest for life. So never have I been more shocked than on the day I found out the devastating news: cancer had taken hold. At best, Jimmy could expect to live for another six months.

But the doctors didn't know Jimmy. This was the most competitive motherfucker I ever met. Not only that, but Jimmy's life was just beginning. He'd met the woman he wanted to grow old with. They'd married and had a daughter, the light of his life, Sierra James. I'll never forget his defiant response to the diagnosis. In classic Jimmy form, he flashed a sly grin and said, "I'm not a statistic, suckas."

By the time Jimmy got his diagnosis, a couple of years after our first trip to Pensacola, I'd closed the door on prioritizing money over living. My friends and family were committed to not taking a minute of the time we had left with Jimmy for granted. So when, in the thick of chemo, Jimmy invited us to take a trip with him to Vegas, it was a no-brainer—we accepted, joining him on a vacation where none of us could match his joyfulness and vigor. A few months later, while the world was locked down by the pandemic, we rode on horseback to the top of a mountain in Jackson Hole. Jimmy may have been poured half a life, but he was savoring every last drop of his cup.

The preciousness of my time with Jimmy was not lost on me when I took that selfie with him. He'd rented a cabin in the Smokies for about forty of his friends. In retrospect, this was his way of bringing together the people he cared to say, "Goodbye and I love you." It was a beautiful time, and when I found the opportunity, I gathered everyone together and turned the camera to commemorate the occasion.

What I didn't realize, though, was that just six weeks later, Jimmy would join me at Matt's funeral—a person also pictured in that photo—who was not diagnosed with cancer, but rather, died due to complications from COVID.

Matt was there for me when I thought I might lose three of my closest friends—Hugo, Jodi, and Tommy—to cancer. It was a dark time, when all of the demons of my youth were coming to the surface, crippling me with depression. And Matt responded just how he always did—with deep presence and unflinching empathy. You'd be hard-pressed to find a more selfless, compassionate human being. A few months after Matt passed, Jimmy followed. It had been three years since Jimmy had been told he had six months to live.

Getting Your Money's Worth

We like to keep death at a distance. We prefer to go through life as if it respects our timing. We take our days for granted, dawdling around until it's convenient to start really going for it and living the good life.

And yet, death has no rhyme and needs no reason. It doesn't ask your permission like an automated phone message—*Do you need more time?* Some people will weigh four hundred pounds and live to ninety, die with a filterless Lucky Strike dangling from their lower lip. Others will eat only organic veggies and grass-fed meat, then drop dead while leading a triathlon before they reach forty. Some will make out like John fucking Wick, unscathed by a thousand bullets whizzing past their heads.

So why bother thinking about it?

Because dying is the cost of living. Yeah, it's expensive—it drains you of everything you ever owned. You can't get around paying it, so you better get your money's worth—you're playing Supermarket Sweep, baby, and the years may be limited, but the shelves are stocked to the heavens.[1] (For those who missed it, this was a game show where suburbanites found a socially acceptable way to loot a grocery store, grabbing whatever they could get their hands on and winning prizes for doing it best.)

> Fear of losing tomorrow steals living today.

In other words, the choices are endless, and they're *yours* to make. So the "dope life" starts with intention and purpose, choosing to take hold of your heart's calling. It's about cultivating the good in and around you, not destroying both through reckless abandon. It's planning as though you'll be here for 100 years, and at the same time, living as if today is all you've got. That is intentionality. That's focus.

---

[1] For those who missed it, this was a game show where suburbanites found a socially-acceptable way to loot a grocery store, grabbing whatever the heaven they could get their hands on and winning prizes for doing it best.

We can live in the now with peace, confidence, and joy even though—no, *because*—we know that tomorrow might not come. That's how Jimmy lived. He was too busy soaking up life to waste a moment fending off death. And trust me, he did it right. Fear of losing tomorrow steals living today. It's true that we don't decide when "the end" is written, but we write every damn page of the adventure that leads up to it. So remember to write one you'll be proud of, whenever the end does come.

Memories That Last

If I had skipped those trips my story would've ended without some of its best chapters. They would've been replaced with: "He stayed home and saved his money."

Riveting.

I would've missed the hours Hugo and I spent out on the beach with *Purple Rain* on repeat, watching the waves roll in and zoning out. I would've missed another chapter of Jodi's and my tradition of finding a karaoke bar and belting out our duet of "Living on a Prayer."

And on the trip I took with Jimmy a few months before he passed, I encountered more bald eagles in a few days than I'd seen in the lifetime that preceded them. Now until I die, I'll see Jimmy's mischievous grin and feel his indomitable spirit whenever one flies overhead.

I doubt Matt imagined that the few hours he offered to a scared and broken friend would have a life-long impact. I'm sure he never imagined the example of his love would last long beyond his passing. It continues to affect not just me, but my children and every hurting person I've visited when I remember how his compassion touched me.

I want to go out like Jimmy.

Someday, each of us will lay on the precipice of the other side, and we'll smile remembering some intimate conversation, some belly laughs we shared. We'll remember the time someone showed up when we needed them and the profound fulfillment we felt when we were there in another's time of need. The money we have will only matter in light of how we use it.

I want to go out like Jimmy. His smile defied pain and mortality. Fear cowered before the fierceness of his love. Nothing could be taken from the man who gave himself with open hands to the world. Jimmy lived life to the fullest, and a story like his lasts long after the last breath of its author.

I don't know what tomorrow holds in my own life. I do know that I've created my most precious memories when I followed my heart in spite of my fears and savored each moment knowing the uncertainty of the next. Do I want it all to end tomorrow? Of course not. But if it does, I know I will leave having lived life. To the fullest.

MAKING LIFE DOPE:

Here's the bad news: our time is limited. Every story has the same closing, "The end." And the good news? Every word until then is a blank canvas awaiting our masterpiece.

> Regret is the bastard child of delay.

So grab your Life is Dope journal or workbook and take the time to reflect on these important questions:

- If my time were to expire today, what would I look back on with regret?
  - What missed opportunities, unspoken words, or unfulfilled dreams would stand out in the story of my life?
- Acknowledge the finite nature of time:
  - Consider what actions, words, or dreams you've left unexplored.
  - What regrets might you have if today were your last?
- Identify the common themes that recur in your thoughts and remain unaddressed.
  - What is one theme you could make a priority starting now?
- Imagine waking up on the other side of reality after your last sleep.
  - Who is the first person that comes to mind that you wish you had shared more with? Reach out and express your feelings to them while you have the chance.
- Consider you have only five more hours. What would you do with this time?

So go, tend to your unfinished business. Don't wait for a eulogy to let someone know how much they mean to you. Forgive, ask for forgiveness. Unload your baggage like your soul depends on it.

> *Legacy is finding pride in being true to yourself as you live your dopest life.*

We don't choose the timeline, and regret is the bastard child of delay. Legacy, though—that's the joy borne of a life not just contemplated and spoken but lived into existence. Legacy is awakening to your power, no longer denying your soul's deepest desires. Legacy is finding pride in being true to yourself as you live your dopest life.

SAVE TIME:
Use the official Life Is Dope workbook and more by visiting MichaelAnthonyTV.com/LifeIsDope or scanning this QR code.
It's 100% free!
And if you already did and are loving it, be sure to tag me on social @michaelanthonytv

STORY 10

Four-Letter Words

> *We can turn our heart through the words we say*
> *Speak life, speak life*
> *To the deadest darkest night*
> *When the sun won't shine and you don't know why*
> **—Toby Mac, "Speak Life"**

There are some words that I won't let anybody get away with using in my fuckinghousehold. I don't give a damn what the excuse is. Oh, you say you can think of a better way to say that shit? Bitch, please!

Some words are just too foul for me to tolerate. Use them on a regular basis, and they'll poison you from the inside out, make a mess of your emotions, and sabotage your actions. They're also flat-out dishonest. They distort the reality of who you are and the world around you.

> On this night, money was no issue.

"What about all the filth you've been spouting?" you might be thinking. Fair question, but I'm not talking about the words that'll earn you detention in school or a scolding from your grandma. I'm talking about the ones that'll fuck you up in the game of life.

So today, kids, I'm going to share a few tales from my own life that taught me what the *real* four-letter words are, the sneaky ones that'll steal the joy from the most prim and proper among us. Now buckle up, because this shit's about to get real, and read the following three words with caution because these fuckers are evil: *Try*, *should*, and *can't*.

There is No *Try*

Whether Dad had gotten a promotion or raise, I don't recall, but I do remember that, on this night, money was no issue. And Dad was taking us to Red Lobster.

All was right in the world. It was me, my parents, and my boy, Alvin. Alvin and I had just joined the wrestling team, and while my parents tried to decide which gut-busting fried entree to order, Alvin and I talked about the match we had coming up.

Both of us were apprehensive about it—on top of the general discomfort of being fifteen years old, we were both new to wrestling. Before us loomed hand-to-hand combat in spandex singlets that left no question as to who had come further in his physical development.

"Well, are you gonna win?" Mom must've sensed our concern because this was a subtle cue to cut the bullshit. "Well, I'm gonna try," I answered. I wasn't even sure I wanted to wrestle. It felt good to talk to Alvin about it—he was in the same boat—but I immediately wanted my mom to drop it. She was raising the stakes, and I was committed to being half-committed.

> "Try and pick that up."

Unfortunately, she wasn't about to let me off that easily. "Do something for me," she said, sliding her fork off the edge of the table and onto the floor. "Try and pick that up." *Uh, what the heck, ok.* I played along and snatched up the fork, hoping this lesson would be a short one.

"No, *try* to pick it up," she said. "I didn't say to pick it up, I said try to." So she threw the fork back down on the ground, and I did my best impression of a person born without depth perception trying and failing to reach the fork on the floor. She let this go on for what must've been ten full seconds before repeating her instruction: "Try to pick it up!" Whatever, ok. So I picked it up again. And she corrected me. Again. *Oh, for fuck's sake.* By this point, I was annoyed.

Much to Alvin's dismay, she turned her attention to him. "Try to pick it up," she said, throwing the fork back down to the ground. "I'm staying out of this," he said with a laugh. "I don't know what to do." My mom wasn't going to let him off that easily, but she did take the cue to wrap it up. So she clarified her instruction: "All right, pick it up." So Alvin grabbed the fork, which by now had far exceeded the five-second rule, and returned it to the table.

"What is 'try'? There is no trying." Mom wasn't a Star Wars fan, but she did apparently share some of the wisdom that has turned Yoda into a meme many times over. "We either do or we don't," she added, her eyes shifting between her young Jedis. I wasn't big into Star Wars, either, so this was the first time I'd heard this concept.

Nevertheless, I got the message loud and clear: "Trying" implies we might not be "good enough" to win. When we say, "I'll try," we unwittingly send the message to our unconscious that we're failing when, in fact, we may well be in the middle of winning. She could see that this wasn't a mindset that would set us up for success.

Ultimately, success comes through doing, even when the journey is longer or harder than expected. Mom was highlighting the importance of acknowledging the effort and progress in the midst of challenge, rather than framing it as failure. She could hear us wavering in our commitment, preparing our egos for the possibility of not meeting our own or others' expectations.

I see this waffling all the time among uncommitted entrepreneurs. I call them "wantrepreneurs". They're not sure they'll make it. Because they can't see the entire staircase, they linger at the bottom, planning, and second-guessing when they could get stepping. Their lack of conviction about the destination ensures a half-hearted commitment. Those who have a vision in their mind and a fire in their belly don't entertain the idea of just trying. They proceed with life-or-death urgency because realizing their vision is their life's purpose. Failure is not an option.

So how could we truly give our all to winning, without self-protection? With commitment—*I will do the work, and I won't give up. I will give 100% in order to succeed. No excuses. No backing out.*

Setting your intention makes you accountable to yourself. It takes guts.

> "I'll try" gives you permission to minimize your personal power and play small.

"I'll try" achieves the opposite. "I'll try to make it to your party." We've heard it before. Those are the words of a flake, the prelude to a cop-out. "I'll try" gives you permission to minimize your personal power and play small. It grants license to bitching about your lack of success in life. After all, "You tried."

For those who choose in advance, though, the ones who've decided what they will and won't do, 'failing' is just one part of growth. There's no need to complain when success eludes the doer. It's recognized as a new obstacle and lesson en route to victory.

The winners either find a way to make it or have the strength to say they won't do it in the first place, but either way, they don't lie to themselves or others. The flakes miss out on the party. The winners, though—they find a way to make it.

Stop Should-ing on Yourself

I'm not a 5 a.m.'er, and thank heavens I've reached a stage in life when I don't need to be. There was a season, though, when the blare of the 4:45 a.m. alarm was my daily call to battle.

> I'm not a 5 a.m.'er.

I'd made a pact with myself: *I would get up at 4:45, no matter what, go straight to the gym, and head to work from there.*

No "try." I *would* conquer my innate hatred of early rising in pursuit of physical fitness because that's what was necessary. This wasn't just about getting in shape—it was about establishing a new identity, the kind I'd need to accomplish what I'd set out to do.

For a while, I powered through resistance, defying the sinister whispers coaxing me to stay under the warm cocoon of my sheets… until one day, I caved.

Arriving at the gym late for the first time since I'd decided to turn over a new leaf, I felt such disgust that you would've thought I'd just shit myself on the pull-up bar. Well, in fact, I'd done something with a similar effect, which is why I now call it "shoulding on yourself."

The barrage of self-criticism as I walked into an almost empty gym was merciless. *You should have gotten up at 4:45, you lazy fuck!* The tirade glossed over the reality—this was my first tardy to my first consistent gym effort in years.

And it only snowballed from there. *You showed up late, and you're STILL being a lazy ass,* I thought. *You should be working much harder.* Well, of course I was dragging. By this point, I wasn't just late, but I'd also taken a beat down at my own hand—not the ideal mindset for an inspired workout.

> Should-ing wasn't motivating, it was soul-crushing.

This cycle was really nothing new. Any time I uttered "I should," I unwittingly embraced the identity of a person who "should" do things but doesn't. The phrase implied that I was not accepting myself as enough, and this belief reinforced every time I failed to meet whatever self-imposed standards I insisted I *should* be doing. It was as if there were two sides of me: the parent who said I was only worthy if I was perfect and the child doomed to slip up. The result? A cycle of despair and self-loathing.

This should-ing wasn't motivating, it was soul-crushing. And it also opened the door for excuses that became self-fulfilling prophecies. "I should" established the ethical standards, and the "but" that followed accepted an identity that ensured I'd fail. *You should have gotten up when you said you would, but you didn't because you're a failure.* No compassion, no encouragement, and no room for imperfection and grace. If I couldn't be perfect, then that was proof: *I failed. I am a failure.*

> Real motivation comes from a place of self-love, not self-criticism.

On that particular morning, though, a subtle and significant shift began to unfold within me. Was this really about the gym, or was it symptomatic of something deeper? Between going to the gym, going to work, and raising two kids, I'd been working my ass off. I returned home every night completely spent. That morning, it seemed my body and mind had conspired against me, refusing to get out of bed. Or were they trying to help?

Those additional fifteen minutes weren't a sign of defeat—they were an act of self-kindness. They were a small concession to the harsh demands I had been placing on my body and mind.

I'd been viewing getting up early to work out as some moral imperative when, in reality, it was a commitment made out of love for myself. How was getting up at 4:45 a.m. benefiting me? By allowing me time to exercise, I improved my energy, my longevity, and my self-image.

Beneath the steaming pile of shoulds, I'd buried the truth: *I want to improve my fitness because it will enhance my self-esteem. I will exercise regularly because I deserve my own effort.*

Above the clanging of weights, the faint echo of music, and the shouted self-judgments and accusations, I realized that I was here to create the health I deserved. I was here because I owed it to myself to struggle against my old ways and forge something new.

This wasn't just about hitting the gym. It was about recognizing my worth, about understanding that self-care isn't selfish—it's essential. And so, as I geared up for another set, it dawned on me: real motivation comes from a place of self-love, not self-criticism.

From that day on, my approach to fitness—and life—changed. Instead of punishing myself for what I hadn't done, I began to celebrate what I was doing. Each step on the treadmill became a step towards self-respect. Each lift of the weights was a lift to my spirits. I was no longer striving for my goals because I "should." I was doing it because I loved myself.

I realized there and then: should-ing on myself wasn't serving any purpose. It wasn't motivating. It was debilitating, like the no-good, bullshitting cousin of "try." *I should be in better shape. I'll try to start working out.*

It was time to change the narrative from a punishing "should" to an empowering "want." I decided it was far more beneficial to embrace *the truth* than to be stifled by shame.

When you shift your focus to the benefits, you shift from being someone deserving of shame to someone worthy of love. When you catch yourself stacking "shoulds" and "shouldn'ts," pause and ask: *how is shoulding all over myself benefitting me?*

It's far more beneficial to speak the truth in power than to smother your power in shame. Here's a more empowering perspective—how would your life look if you affirmed that you are worthy of a level of well-being that you haven't yet achieved? What if you replaced all those "shoulds" with the benefits, the good things in life you want and haven't attained yet? Yes, this means loving yourself

> Pause and ask: how is shoulding all over myself benefitting me?

enough to keep going—not beating yourself up so badly about the past that you end up hobbling into the future on crutches.

The Most Sinister Four-Letter Word of All

"Can we go to the fair, Daddy?"

With her little brother, Matthew, standing over her shoulder, my seven-year-old daughter Mikayla looked up at me with starry-eyed anticipation, hoping her request would pay off. It was obvious that this had been discussed in advance and that Mikayla had mustered the courage to ask, but before she could even get the "Daddy" part out, I'd dismissed the possibility.

"No, we can't."

I'd been on the road for six of the last twelve months, and now I was on full-time daddy duty every weekend of the summer while Sarah was working. I was tired. Plus, I'd been to the fair growing up—it sucked.

In reality, though, all of those rationalizations were a smokescreen for one loud, hard-line verdict that led me to quash Mikayla's hopes of riding a Ferris wheel: *we can't afford it.*

If you've ever been poor, you know how quickly you can do the kind of math that adds up to "can't." "Three entry fees, no telling how many ride tickets. And they'll probably want me to get on those wallet-draining, thirty-second rides with them. Then there's the five-dollar hot dogs they bought for a quarter apiece. Call it a hundred bucks? Screw that."

As soon as the word "can't" left my lips, something weird happened. As I stood there watching my kids' eyes shift from anticipation to disappointment, a vivid image popped into my head—red bricks dropping like Tetris pieces to block out my mind.

> For the first time, I challenged my assumptions

The visual of my source of all potential creativity and abundance being walled off scared the shit out of me. It sent me into a state of fight or flight, and my first instinct was to fight. I realized that the word "can't" had just shut my brain down, defaulting to a mindset that saw no alternative to scarcity. And with all of that unconscious programming suddenly conscious, all I could think was, *No!*

Just then, it was like the bricks fell, flooding me with more information than I could process at once. I started channeling my inner Zig Ziglar—*I know I'm capable of finding alternatives.* And I began to wonder: how long had I let my brain be hijacked in the way I'd just witnessed?

For the first time, I challenged my assumptions: *Is it truly impossible for us to go to the fair? Could I not find SOME way to get SOME money if my life depended on it?*

Maybe, just maybe, it wasn't a matter of "can't" but "won't." In reality, the money it would cost to attend the fair was allocated for more immediate needs. Sure, we could've followed the American way and used a credit card. But creating debt for the sake of a good time wouldn't have been beneficial either. On top of the financial aspect was the fact that wading through crowds and spinning around to the point of nausea held no appeal for me.

I thought of all the "can'ts" that were holding my life hostage—I *can't* get another job. I *can't* earn money. I *can't* live in peace. And why couldn't I do all of these things? Because I was a slave to the most sinister four-letter word of all: *Can't.*

I was accepting defeat and the identity of a victim. And worst of all, I realized that I was crippling my children's minds and spirits. Mikayla had hope, and here I was telling her it was impossible. I recognized that unless I dismantled these beliefs in myself, I'd pass their weight to my children.

> *Unless I dismantled these beliefs in myself,
> I'd pass their weight to my children.*

After I'd replayed the scenario a hundred times in my head, I committed to building my awareness of my use of the word "can't" and replacing it with a more accurate word or phrase every time I caught myself. Determined to prevent "can't" from standing in the way of my children's dreams, I called them over to the kitchen table and leveled with them. "Guys, I understand you want to go to the fair. I would like to take you to the fair. So if we go, here's the challenge." They were wide-eyed, locked into every word I was saying. "That money is going to come from somewhere else. And I don't feel like that's a good use of funds. Mom's out there right now working to earn money for us—for food, clothes, school—things I value more than going to the fair. Mom and I are working really hard for us so that we can have more money in the future."

Then I gave them some alternatives. We could go to the park, go out in the yard, and play in the sprinkler. We could build a fort out of couch cushions or play hide-and-seek in the house. And as I braced for their objections, I kid you not, Mikayla said, "Well then, we don't want to do it." Her little brother, who thought she hung the moon, nodded in agreement. "If it's not good for our family, then I don't want to go." *Holy fuck.* Thankfully, I didn't say that out loud.

And Mikayla wasn't done. As God is my witness, she added, "Dad, if not having enough money is the problem, what if we did something to earn some money?"

I was dumbfounded. She understood what took me a Tetris nightmare to get

> We gave them a twenty-dollar loan and a million-dollar business lesson.

through my thick skull. I could see that she was flowing, and I wasn't about to slow her down.

"What do you have in mind?" I asked. And she gave the same adorable answer as every enterprising kid since the days of black-and-white TV: "Well, we could do like a lemonade stand." Then, from the seat that swallowed his little five-year-old frame, Matthew chimed in: "YEAH!"

So what did we do? We gave them a twenty-dollar loan and a million-dollar business lesson. They'd need a good location and supplies—signage, sugar, real lemons so the customers know they're getting the good stuff. We figured out how much of each we'd need to earn the cost of a night at the fair. All the while, they were chiming in with ideas, which I wrote down, including Mikayla's stroke of genius to set up near a neighbor's garage sale the following weekend.

We made all of the preparations, set up our stand, and the lemonade stand bombed completely.

Nah, just kidding—it *destroyed*. They paid us back our twenty bucks and allotted the rest to buy more supplies. Suddenly, the fair was an afterthought to the lemonade business, which ended up running on and off for another five years. There were arguments along the way. They sometimes questioned the best way to go about things, but the word "can't" never entered into the discussion.

Fuck Around and Find Out

We've been duped. Some of my absolute favorite words have been vilified while the real culprits hide in plain sight. No more. I called these culprits out of hiding, and I urge you to do the same. Your power will grow and the power of these words diminishes each time you look them in the eye and see them for who they really are.

So what is one to do? Take them out of your vocabulary completely. What I'm proposing isn't easy, because they're so easily overlooked.

These words often slip past our awareness—*try, should, can't*—and, in the process, profoundly impact our mindset and actions.

The process of cleaning up my language took about five years of practice before those words stopped sneaking by me undetected. The real transformation began when I actively replaced them with words that mirrored my capacity for growth and creativity. This mindful communication has not only changed my neural pathways—it has also reshaped my emotions and actions. The result? Greater clarity, focus, and a sense of calm and empowerment.

Most of what is celebrated as a dope life nowadays is superficial, a curated facade meant for social media. But the truly dope life—the one filled with meaning, purpose, and genuine happiness—happens beneath the surface. It's built on a foundation of hope and empowerment, nourished by the words we choose to define our experiences and ourselves.

So, let's commit to rewriting our narratives with the words that resonate with our deepest truths and affirm our true power. By doing so, we create a life of richness that is deeply felt and observable. You will, you can, transform every "should" into an act of self-love and a declaration of your deep purpose.

MAKING LIFE DOPE:

Grab your Life Is Dope journal or workbook and do the following to reclaim your dope life:

- If you're should-ing on yourself, how is it benefiting you?
  - Write about how your life is better from the work you're putting in now. (hint: reading this book qualifies as putting in work)
- Identify your four-letter words.
  - Write down some of the words that sneak into your vocabulary and undermine your power.

- Which one gets past you the most?
- Which one do you think does the most damage?
- Decide on replacements.
  - For each word/phrase that you've identified, choose a replacement word/phrase that reflects your power to create, to grow, and to be intentional.

After you've responded to these questions, write out your new words as a list to put by your bed, mirror, fridge, desk, and even the wallpaper on your phone. Make sure they're handy so you can easily practice replacing your old habit words with new phrases that make your life dope!

BONUS:

If you want to dive deeper and save time, grab the official Life Is Dope Accompaniment workbook for free! Visit MichaelAnthonyTV.com/LifeIsDope or scan this QR code. Let me know how your journey is going by tagging me @MichaelAnthonyTV

STORY 11

Design a Life You Don't Need a Vacation From

> *I'm on vacation every single day*
> *'cause I love my occupation*
> *If you don't like your life,*
> *then you should go and change it*
> —**Dirty Heads, "Vacation"**

It was the kind of scene that Instagram dreams are made of—a three-hundred-foot, panoramic expanse of floor-to-ceiling windows that opened to the crystal-blue waters of the Caribbean. So far, this visit to the spa included a full-body massage, a facial, then a shoulder, neck, and scalp massage. Now I was waiting on my first mani-pedi in over a decade.

> *It was one of the saddest moments in my life.*

And there, in the lap of luxury, surrounded by the sublime sounds of singing bowls and bubbling brooks, all I could think of was how badly I wanted to go home to my family. It was one of the saddest moments in my life.

A Chance Meeting

I remember feeling jealous of people who traveled for work and slightly irritated when they complained about it. Oh God, you had to take a first-class flight out to London on business? You poor thing.

The point I was missing, though, is that travel is a bit like opening a birthday gift—tearing it open in a room by yourself isn't as fun as when others are sharing the experience with you. In fact, it gets sadder with every present you open.

That's just how I felt lounging next to the lagoon pool at the Cancun resort, the same place where I'd have that disheartening spa visit a few days later.

I'd been on the grind for three months straight, bouncing from city to city and country to country, organizing speaking events with one titan in the world of business and leadership after another. Each exotic destination blurred into the next and none were capable of replacing the comfort of home.

In a sense, I loved what I did—people left the events full of hope and empowerment. Plus, all of this travel was a dream come true. Even if it was a dream I hadn't thought all the way through. With each stop, we'd feverishly set up for the event, have a few days of talks, then break it all back down, and head out to do it all over again. Sometimes we'd be at a stadium for fifteen thousand attendees, others in a venue of a few hundred at ten thousand dollars a head. This was one of the latter.

Tired and lonely, at another picturesque setting far from home, my trance was interrupted by a friendly voice, "Mind if we join you?"

"Go right ahead," I answered. The couple that took the seat next to me exuded an energy that was the opposite of my current state. They were vibrant and open, light and at the same time palpably enthusiastic. Anyone else, and I would've wished to be left alone. In this case, though, the contagion of their presence shook me from my stupor. Before long, we were deep in conversation.

Obviously, they had spent *a lot* of money to be here. However, they weren't the likeliest of attendees. Three years earlier, he had been a full-time fireman. It was a noble profession and one he took pride in, except for one problem: his income couldn't provide for the lifestyle they desired. They were left with two choices: let go of their dreams of what could be or make the drastic changes necessary to make those dreams a reality.

They had chosen the latter, and here they were, at a five-star resort in paradise, attending a professional development conference that would've cost them six months of salary three years prior. They'd paid their way on discretionary income, with enough left over to bring their nanny along so they could immerse themselves in the week's proceedings while their children were being cared for.

I loved connecting with them and felt genuinely happy for the abundance they were so obviously enjoying. And at the same time, I desperately wanted what they had. I missed my wife and children terribly. I missed my friends. My only connections on the road were surface-level acquaintances who knew Mike the event coordinator, but very little of the man behind the professional.

The couple picked up on my trouble in paradise and began asking about my life. As I shared my story, they related to my longing for more, having gone through their own three-year journey leading up to that moment.

On the last day of the trip, I crossed paths with them again. After some small talk, the former fireman locked eyes with me and asked a pointed question. "What standards in your life are keeping you in a place of discontent?" he asked. "What would have to be true for you to feel like you have what we have?"

"What standards in your life are keeping you in a place of discontent?"

He encouraged me to consider these questions in deciding my path forward. And in the meantime, they offered me a parting gift—$2,500 credit for anything on the spa menu. *Maybe a day of indulgence will calm my restless mind before I wrestle with those questions.* Well, you know how that turned out.

No Vacation Required

About twenty years ago, I read a book in which the author casually mentioned that he reserved three months of vacation per year. Three months of vacation?! I couldn't wrap my head around the idea of taking that much time off of work. This guy's completely out of touch, I thought. That's not realistic for "people like me."

Luckily, I noticed how reflexively I dismissed his suggestion and decided to question myself a bit. *Why* not *people like me?* It occurred to me that by downplaying his reality, I was unwittingly stifling my own potential. So I asked another question, *Why am I not worthy of doing whatever the heaven I want instead of what I'm told for a full 90 days?* And that's when it hit me: *I deserve even more!*

> "What would a life of freedom and contentment look like for you?"

What if you didn't have to wait for vacation to do whatever you wanted? What if the only rules you followed were the ones you fully assented to *or* set yourself? What if you intentionally shaped your daily life to align with your genuine desires so that *every* day felt like a vacation?

In Cancun, when my new friend asked, "What would have to be true for you to feel like you have what we have?" I think what he really meant was, "What would a life of freedom and contentment look like for you?" Sure, he was speaking in part about the sacrifice necessary to get to a better place. Rarely does a life of fulfillment happen without some work on the front end that's worth it because of the payoff on the back end. However, there's a big difference between grinding away endlessly in the hope of finally putting your feet up and living a life where freedom unfolds with every value-affirming choice.

It's no accident that this chapter is called "*Design* a Life You Don't Need a Vacation From." "Design" speaks to intentionality, to doing something with purpose. I am all for busting your ass to get to a better place. What I am adamantly against is busting your ass with zero increase in peace and contentment. And that is the sinister danger of striving without intention—it's entirely possible and tragically common for a person to spend their life climbing a ladder that leads to a wasp's nest.

Sure, I wanted three months of vacation a year. Who doesn't? What I really wanted, though, was a life I didn't need a vacation from.

What's Next?

Two years removed from that trip to Cancun and still inspired by the example of the couple I'd met there, I printed off these words and posted them at my desk so I'd see them while I worked every day: Design a life you don't need a vacation from.

At the same time, I made some major changes to initiate the design process. When I realized my dreams and my vocation were incompatible, I joined Sarah in getting our insurance agency off the ground. And it didn't take long for us to start thriving in the business. After a couple of years, we'd earned four trips from the corporate office and insurance carriers to reward the success of our agency.

On one hand, these trips suggested that my "life design" was right on track. I wasn't opening gifts alone anymore—Sarah joined me in discovering what each destination had to offer, and we also started an annual tradition of taking our kids on one epic family trip, including an international journey every two years.

Fast forward several years since we'd established the traditions inspired by my encounter at the pool.

For nine months, I'd been grinding towards a singular accomplishment. What accomplishment, you ask? Ironically enough, *a vacation*. This wasn't just any vacation, though. It was *the* vacation… to a destination so momentous that it has since slipped my memory— some five-star resort where people spend a thousand dollars to stay the night and fifty bucks for a plate of eggs the next morning. Unimaginably gorgeous, gratuitously extravagant.

Now I can tell you today that the issue wasn't busting my ass for nine months. In fact, I would go back and do the same thing again to earn that trip and the lessons I learned as a result. Because what I learned was that I had my perspective all wrong.

By the time I reached the finish line to earn *the* trip, I'd burned out my engine and the tank was empty. For most of that time, I had blinders on, oblivious to all but the end goal. I fully created the fate of eliminating any pleasure and suffering my way to earning that trip.

I'd been subscribing to what I now call an "events-focused" view of life: *When I get/do/achieve 'x', then I'll be happy.* There are extreme versions of this—extreme, yet far from uncommon—*I'm going to work hard in this job I hate for twenty-five years, then retire with a gold watch*. Then there's something more akin to what I was doing: *I'm going to work my ass off, then I'll get the reward of the evening/ weekend/next vacation*. When you focus on an event and ignore the journey, you live on a never-ending hamster wheel. There's no lasting fulfillment, only "Next!"

I spent that vacation troubled in my spirit and perpetually preoccupied with how fast my "reward" was slipping through my fingers. And predictably, I returned tired and empty, with none of the promised renewal realized. I'd managed to ignore the message that lived a few inches from my nose for nine months—I wasn't designing a life I didn't need a vacation from. I was designing a life that gave me some great vacations. Meanwhile, I'd been neglecting 95% of the journey for the 5% left over, and I'd used up all of the enthusiasm necessary to truly savor the reward.

Don't get me wrong—I'm in full support of busting ass for a worthy goal. During that season, though, the alternatives weren't "work hard" or "sit on my ass and call it enjoying the journey." They were "work hard and sacrifice any semblance of self-care and gratitude" or "work hard and appreciate the continual movement toward a tomorrow that's better than today—and eventually, a vacation too." There was a wealth of rewards that I completely overlooked along the way—triumphs over obstacles, personal growth, and countless opportunities for genuine relaxation squandered due to preoccupation with the destination.

So once again, I had to regroup and reconsider the life I was building. I'd come a long way from that guy staring off into space by the lagoon pool. And yet, this wasn't it. I was looking past the love of my job to focus on the next carrot I was chasing.

> I had to regroup and reconsider the life I was building.

And the problem was, this approach was working—even though it wasn't. I was earning the rewards and missing out on the true prize of *every* day as a vacation.

The pivotal question that inspired my transformation was this: how do I truly *live*, every day, not just during those trips every six to nine months, but in all the moments in between? That is where life is lived. The real trip is the one that happens between vacations.

Be Here on the Way There

There's a real danger in arriving at your dream destination only to discover that you overlooked the true treasures of the journey itself. I know—I've lived it and learned that there's another way.

Fulfillment doesn't have to be postponed. The genuine treasures, the singular source of all significant moments in life, lie in embracing the present.

The trip I took to Cancun, and the one Sarah and I earned a few years later, were the stuff of internet sizzle. Often, though, what sparkles on social media lacks substance. When your everyday existence reflects your values and the things that bring you fulfillment, contentment, peace, joy—that's the life of substance.

By all means, fashion a vision vivid and profound enough to draw you forward. It is just as crucial that you choose a worthwhile direction as it is that you follow your chosen path in a spirit of reflection. What I firmly oppose is losing sight of the journey, and discarding all of the experiences and growth that occur between the starting point and the destination.

> Fashion a vision vivid and profound enough to draw you forward.

When you live like that, you search for purpose in external things, relying on diversions, temporary indulgences, or the promise of a coveted destination to fill the growing void. The alternative is acting out of self-respect and embracing the pressures along the way with self-love. When you live in this manner, you fully inhabit yourself during the journey, upon reaching your destination, and after you depart.

Content And Never Satisfied

There is a difference between being content and being satisfied. Before I understood the importance of focusing on the journey, I was neither content nor satisfied. Today, I am content, and I am unsatisfied. Will I ever be satisfied? I hope not!

> There is a difference between being content and being satisfied.

One of my guiding principles is to ensure that I make tomorrow better than today. This mindset keeps me from settling, as I'm aware that greater joys are ahead. I greet each day savoring what is, with faith in all that can be if only I'm willing to go and get it. By living each day determined to make the most of all that I've been given, I know I'll reach the last of my days filled with gratitude and the knowledge that I took nothing for granted.

Shortly after encountering that author's claim about taking a three-month annual vacation, I went on my first cruise. Overlooking the Atlantic Ocean from the deck of that ship, I made a promise to myself: someday, I'll take a cruise that circumnavigates the world, returning to the very port from which I depart.

By the time you read this, I will have made good on that promise. And it'll be so much more rewarding than the trip I imagined. I'll leave that port with a heart full of joy and a conscience unburdened, knowing I didn't forfeit my contentment on the journey towards my goal.

Yes, I'm realizing the life of abundant vacations that seemed so impossible when I read about it years ago. More importantly, I'm learning to embody what that couple demonstrated to me: a life exists where vacations are not an escape but the cherry on top of an already sweet day-to-day existence. That's the essence of the dope life. The lines between work and play blur, because each day is infused with passion, purpose, and presence.

> *A life exists where vacations are not an escape but the cherry on top.*

MAKING LIFE DOPE:

Life doesn't just transform at the snap of your fingers. Far from it. It starts with setting standards that reflect the value you place on yourself. Life gives us not just what we ask, but what we demand of it. By the same token, it will give us as little as we're willing to settle for.

The question I had to ask myself in those formative encounters is the same one I challenge you to ask yourself. So grab your Life Is Dope journal or workbook and reflect on the following:

- Why not you?
    - If others are living the life you desire, what makes you any less worthy of living that life yourself?
    - What would have to change to make your dream a reality?
- What emotions come up from that first question?
    - Does the meaning you give to these emotions serve you?
    - And if not, how could you flip the coin to create an empowering story?
- Now, what if you began to take your heart's desires seriously, insisting on precisely what it yearns for?
- What if you committed to persevering long enough to TAKE the success you dream of?

Challenge the limits you've placed on yourself. Demand more from life, not just in the grand milestones but in the simple, everyday moments. Remember, the real trip is the life you're living right now. Make it dope.

BONUS:

Have you gone to MichaelAnthonyTV.com/LifeIsDope yet to get your free copy of the official Life Is Dope Accompaniment workbook and access some pretty dope music playlists?
It's totally free, so what are ya waiting for?
Let me know how your life is becoming more dope.
Tag me @MichaelAnthonyTV

STORY 12

Your #1 Investment

This is your life
Are you who you want to be?
This is your life
Is it everything you dreamed
—Switchfoot, "This Is Your Life"

Over the course of my adult years, I have invested over $350,000 in books, therapy, and business, leadership, and self-development conferences, all for... *myself*. Seriously. I did the math.

At times, the money I was investing in personal growth seemed crazy to others. But I was curious. What would happen if I kept putting a little something into my personal growth account? What if I kept working on the one thing I will always have with me, no matter what? Would continually betting on myself be worth it? I had a hunch but didn't know for sure. So I kept going and doubling down—on me.

And for the first time in my life, after so many years of struggle, I logged on and there it was, right on the screen. Proof that this bet had paid off.

At forty years old, I was a millionaire.

Investing in Yourself

My and Sarah's insurance business was on fire. Every month, I'd close the books and discover that this one was better than the last—growing profits, new agents crushing it, and processes in place to ensure we'd continue to fire on all cylinders.

Profits were high enough for us to pay ourselves a comfortable salary, a luxury many entrepreneurs never have the chance to experience. We had a growing stockpile in our personal and business emergency funds, and exponentially more discretionary income to invest back into the business. I felt frickin amazing.

And then, my brain would jerk the curtains shut and black out all that sunshine. I was stuck in this self-defeating negative feedback loop. *What business do you have feeling excited? You're almost forty, and you aren't setting any money aside for retirement. What kind of person doesn't plan for their family's future? You're not winning, you're failing. You're a failure and a fraud.*

It's no accident that I ended up spending a solid chunk of my pre-entrepreneurship adulthood working for a company whose CEO built his massive success on preaching the importance of saving your pennies and eliminating debt. I'd watched my parents' financial struggles steal any semblance of freedom they might have had, and I'd determined at a very early age to not follow in their footsteps.

When I took on that education job, I was doing the best I could do on the modest income I was making. I hadn't managed to pay off our house yet. We didn't have many assets, aside from good old Mater McQueen.

But we were debt-free, and one of the steps the man-in-charge advocated was saving for retirement as soon as your debts were paid off. And so, following the blueprint, l opened a retirement account and took advantage of employee match. Each month, when this money was taken out of my paycheck, I felt deep comfort and pride. Sure, I didn't enjoy that there was less money to live on, but I did take deep pleasure in being "responsible" for building toward the future.

And now I was a failure because I was no longer an "employee" who enjoyed the benefit of getting a couple extra grand a year of kickback from my employer? I was a fraud now because I wasn't relegating a portion of our revenue to an IRA or a 401(k)?

As sound as the logic of that script had been in my former life, it was time for a revised second edition. I asked myself, *Okay, what's the best use of that money? What am I really beating myself up over when it comes to not putting money "into retirement?"*

> It was time for a revised second edition.

It occurred to me that holding off on a retirement fund to invest in myself and our business wasn't so different from a person investing in shares of a company. *If* Steve Jobs buys shares of Apple, I thought, *he's just investing in himself.* And what if I'd invested $10,000 in Apple when it first started? Would I have wanted Steve Jobs to take that money and set some of it aside for retirement or put all of it into himself and the company?

The answer was blatantly obvious. I'd actually be downright pissed off if he took my money and put it into anything *but* himself and Apple. If I bet on Apple to become the company I believed it could be, then what would give Apple the best fighting chance at that happening? Steve investing in himself and what he was building.

How do the ultra-wealthy typically get where they are? Usually by going really fucking deep on one thing—the cash cow that they then leverage and diversify. Sure there are the "Millionaire Next Door" millionaires who invest their modest employee salary in broad funds and eventually build up to that next zero on their net worth. But entrepreneurs—the ones that makeup 88% of the world's millionaires—get there on the backs of their own bread and butter. Steve Jobs did it with Apple. Mark Cuban founded the video portal

Broadcast.com in 1995 and sold it to Yahoo four years later for $5.7 billion. And then there was Andrew Carnegie, who concentrated on steel production in the early industrial age, and then sold his company for $480 million in 1901. He became one of the richest men ever, then diversified this sum—the equivalent to billions today—into philanthropy, literally building the framework for public libraries across the U.S.

Now, by channeling our profits back into the growth of our business, Sarah and I were betting on our ability to grow and manage our enterprise effectively. Just as Jobs's investment in Apple wasn't just about financial returns but about believing in and building something transformative, our investment in our business represented a profound act of faith in our joint potential. I wasn't an employee anymore. I wasn't putting my bets on anyone or anything else. I was investing in something I believed in—Sarah and I.

Misguided Priorities

The average payment for a new car in 2023 was right around $750. Well, when you roll up in your friends or family's driveway to show off your shiny new car, is anyone going to say something negative about your purchase? More than likely, no one is going to bat an eye. They'll probably be thrilled for you.

Well, what if you invested that same amount, month after month, in the driver? Let's say you put somewhere in the neighborhood of ten grand a year toward investing in yourself while driving a piece of shit car. You see where I'm going? Those same family and friends who celebrated your "investment" in a car that's depreciating in value might have a cross word or two to say about the investment in yourself—an investment that will continue to sparkle and compound years after the money is paid out.

Well, I drove a car most would consider a piece of shit for years. I drove that fucker everywhere–conferences, therapy sessions, the gym—anywhere that led to self-improvement and nurturing the talents to their true potential. Sometimes, I was embarrassed, like the time me and Mater came face to face with the perfect suburban dad in his perfect car. Sometimes, I felt like I stood out from the crowd. Sometimes, I wanted to say "fuck it," and stop delaying gratification. I deserved a new car.

> Sometimes, I wanted to say "fuck it," and stop delaying gratification.

No, what I deserved was the strength of will to wait for the real payoff. Do I regret not splurging on a fancy car back when I was making thirty-five grand, driving Mater McQueen, and instead investing in my own growth? Consider this: the same guy who made those choices later paid cash for a Tesla Model S and is now financially independent. So do I regret it—what do you think?

Me Inc.

What's more worth it to you? The car or the driver? Immediate or ultimate gratification? Which has greater potential to transform your life? Which will lead to more lasting fulfillment?

Well, Warren Buffett, possibly the greatest investor of all time says this: "Invest in as much of yourself as you can; you are your own biggest asset by far."

The same goes for your business: "I always invest my own money in the companies that I create," said Elon Musk.

It also pertains to personal development: "An investment in knowledge pays the best interest," said Benjamin Franklin.

And if those endorsements don't convince you, consider the wise words of Pitbull: "Don't be afraid to lose. Listen. And always invest in yourself."

When Pitbull talks, you listen.

Ultimately, it's your choice—you can either emulate the broke guy with the fancy car or the experts who *could* drive a new one off the lot every week. The former invested in the ego. The latter invested in the self. As CEO of Me Inc., it's not your responsibility to manage the impressions of your friends, your mom, and your neighbors. Your responsibility is to ensure that the CEO is focused and fit, equipped to fully offer their gifts to their business and the world.

The people who question that perspective are typically the ones who at some point opted to give up on themselves and stick with the program. They have the nice car, the nice things—and they're stagnant. If you're one of those people, it's not too late. If you're the one who's controlled by the opinion of those people, fuck 'em. Don't let your detractors distract you from your central responsibility—*you*. Impression-management is not your job. Your job is to know where you're going and make sure you're equipped to get there.

> Impression-management is not your job.

The Best Bet

All of us in the developed world have a massive obstacle to contend with. We're born into a world of rampant consumption and trained to follow suit. For consumers, saving and investment are afterthoughts. We're not here to delay gratification, we're here to expedite it. This machine we're born into counts on us for its survival. And yet, what if the very thing holding you back from the life you desire is your unwillingness to invest in yourself?

> Most people are broken, even if they're not broke.

The sad reality is that most people are broken, even if they're not broke. They have a low ceiling of hope for their lives. They fill the narrow confines of their world with instant gratification to fill the void of their existence. They furiously scroll for the dopamine hit that will distract them from the hopelessness of the life they've settled for. They consume whatever will offer an interruption to the joyless reality of living a life inferior to the one they feel capable of creating.

The key to investing in yourself is loving and seeing value in yourself. Valuable assets are those that deliver a lasting return. Not a dopamine hit. Granted, there are investments that deliver that, too.

When it comes to investing in yourself, it's important to consider the return. Will this experience still be delivering in three months, six months, a year, five years, a decade? Maybe that vacation you're considering meets the criteria. Maybe that designer coat *is* actually an investment because you feel like a million dollars every time you put it on.

Invest in yourself. And don't eat your seed. Take the money you earn to grow yourself, not to live a lavish lifestyle. With discipline, the time will come when you can choose to partake in those luxuries with the same discipline that got you there. Case in point—I paid for my Tesla with cash.

The car doesn't make me, I make it. I don't need a Tesla to feel good about myself, because I did the hard work and invested in loving myself when I was driving a beater. So when the time came, buying my Tesla felt symbolic, the realization of a dream that would've seemed impossible a few years prior. I'd already found my power—the power to make an impact on the world that doesn't depend on what I drive.

Besides, I am still technically living below my means. Are you? Life presents us with two options: nurture your growth or spend to silence the discomfort of unfulfillment. The option you choose says all you need to know about how much you value your growth and believe in your potential.

Putting Your Money Where Your Mouth Is

Investing in yourself is never convenient. Early on, it pretty much always felt like I "didn't have the money." But here's the thing: the investment you make in yourself will earn you buckets of money in the long run.

When I say "invest in yourself," I'm talking about more than just throwing cash around. Over the years, I've funneled significant funds into books, therapy sessions, and professional seminars. This might seem extravagant to some, but guess what? It's paying off, big time. And don't think it's just about dollar bills. Time, focus, a listening ear from a mentor—that's currency, too.

But back to my net worth. Did it feel good to see that seventh figure? Hell yeah, it did, even if the number was arbitrary. It was a few thousand bucks more than the month before, which added an extra zero to my net worth.

Except, for me, that zero meant something more. Twenty years, fifteen of which I earned no more than fifty-thousand dollars in a year. Fifty-thousand dollars. Do you know how far fifty grand goes with a family of four? The answer is month-to-month if you're lucky.

For the majority of those twenty years, the amount I was investing into my personal growth seemed absurd. And yet, I'd proven my doubters wrong, including the one who'd expressed more doubt over the course of those twenty years than any other—me. I'd reached this once impossible milestone and could finally take my foot off the gas, right?

> Time, focus, a listening ear from a mentor—that's currency, too.

Nope! If I was once a believer in investing in yourself, now I am an evangelist. Today, I put well into six figures a year into my development. Expensive? Well, I can tell you this from experience—ignorance and stagnation are far more expensive. I may sound out of touch and insensitive to those struggling to pay their bills. I get it. I've been there.

Take the first Tony Robbins event I attended. Yes, I'd worked my ass off and scraped together every spare penny to get there. And when it was time to settle the bill, I repeated the old, tired narrative to myself—the same one I hear echoed by would-be coaching clients, punctuated by the most sinister of the four-letter words: I can't afford that. Luckily, despite my hemming and hawing, I ended up going for free—my employer stepped in to cover the registration fee, chalking it up to "ongoing education."

Then, less than six months later, under the same financial constraints but with a newfound appreciation for the invaluable experience, I attended the same event in a different city. Only this time, I picked up the tab—for myself, Sarah, and two of our best friends. The whole "I can't afford it" bit was bullshit. The only thing that had changed was my mindset. And that's why I don't buy it when I hear it from others—I peddled bullshit, so I can spot it a mile away.

MAKING LIFE DOPE:

Now, it's your turn to confront and break through your own barriers. Grab that Life Is Dope journal or workbook again and consider the following:

- Getting honest with yourself.
    - Identify when you're using "I can't afford it" as an excuse.
    - What are the underlying reasons? Fear, comfort in the status quo, a lack of interest? Something else?
    - Instead of focusing on how it "can't" work, what would have to be true for it to happen?
  - List these down. These are the seeds of action and growth for you to take, starting now!
- Making a small investment in yourself.
    - Decide on a small, meaningful way to invest in your self-development today. It doesn't have to be financial. It could be time, effort, changing habits, etc.
- Write down your investment plan.
    - List a few ways you can start investing in yourself today, this week, this month, and this year. (hint: libraries and YouTube are free)
- Establishing accountability
    - Text someone to tell them what you're doing. Just remember, they don't hold you accountable—*you* hold you accountable. Sharing is a support in the process of forming a new habit. So, go on...put the book down and send that text!

Everyone has to start somewhere. Recognizing the value in yourself is the first step toward making that investment. This action serves as a testament to your self-belief and intentional living.

Go ahead—bet on yourself. You're the best investment you'll ever make.

> **BONUS:**
> Dive deeper by using the official Life Is Dope Accompaniment workbook, music playlists and more for free, by visiting MichaelAnthonyTV.com/LifeIsDope or scanning this QR code. And if you already did this, tag me @MichaelAnthonyTV so I can give you a virtual high five!

STORY 13

The Greatest Gifts Are Those You Give

Don't you worry, don't you worry, child
See Heaven's got a plan for you
—Swedish House Mafia, "Don't You Worry Child"

I meandered around the showroom floor, feeling like 8-Mile-era Eminem on the brink of a rap battle: "My palms are sweaty, knees weak, arms are heavy. There's vomit on my sweater already, mom's spaghetti…" JK. For real, though, my palms were sweating like a sixth grader at his first middle school dance when the salesman approached. Before he could ask me to dance, I explained to him why I was there.

A few years short of forty, I picked up a biography of Elon Musk. My takeaway from the book was that the Tesla should have been impossible. The average internal combustion engine vehicle has about 2,000 moving parts. Tesla has a few less than that—about 1,880 less.

> *I saw the impossible made possible. I saw myself.*

By the time I finished the book, my imagination was ignited. There are cars, and then there are Teslas—a completely reimagined and redesigned mode of transportation. From that day on, whenever I saw a Tesla, I didn't see a cool car or status symbol. I saw the impossible made possible. I saw myself.

As someone who had to overcome a childhood of poverty and continual trauma, I could relate to defying all the odds. I wanted one. No. Fuck that. Some day, I *would* have one.

My purpose wasn't to make a purchase on that day, though. Rather, it was an affirmation of my vision. As much as I wanted to believe I'd have a Tesla someday, I was dealing with some very convincing feelings of unworthiness. The feelings were so strong, in fact, that I felt like I was going to puke just driving to the dealership. Nevertheless, I knew what I had to do. I was there to face these feelings head-on. I was there to affirm my conviction through action.

"You know what," the salesman said as he began to make his way towards the offices in the back of the showroom. "I have something for you. Hold on just a minute." He returned holding a blank note card. It featured a full-color image of a red Tesla Model S, which he explained was one of the last three cards of its kind.

Every morning thereafter, I was greeted by the image of the Model S, providing inspiration for years as I worked at my desk. No other material possession could match the inspiration that the Model S offered me.

Turning Forty

"Hey, what do you want for your birthday?" Sarah was thinking big for my big 4-0. Meanwhile, I was at a complete loss. Business was booming, and "work" involved frequent travel to exotic resorts with my family. My kids were happy and healthy. I was content. My life was dope.

"I don't know," I finally answered. "I got nothin'."

And that was that, I was off the hook. But being the amazing human Sarah is, she didn't let it go that easily. A few days passed, then she came to me with a declaration: "We're gonna get you a Tesla for your birthday."

I was dumbfounded. Instantly, I recalled the vow I'd made to only buy a Tesla if I was a millionaire and could pay in cash. Then, almost simultaneously, it dawned on me—*I am a millionaire and I have the cash.*

Still, something was off, and I couldn't quite put my finger on it. Heck, there was a part of me that didn't *want* to put my finger on it. I'd crossed the finish line I'd drawn out years ago. But there was no denying it—my heart was pulling me in some other direction.

> There was no denying it—my heart was pulling me in some other direction.

Sarah knew how much I'd thought about this car, so she kept pushing me to uncover my resistance. Why did I keep brushing her off? Did I not feel worthy? In all honesty, that seemed the most obvious explanation—feelings of unworthiness were nothing new to me—and yet I knew this was something different.

And so, I did what I still do when faced with a tangled impasse in my mind—I sat down with my journal and began to write.

By the time I put down my pen, it was as plain as day. As much as I'd downplayed it, this fortieth birthday meant more than I had let on. This would be a day to remember. The way I chose to commemorate it would shape whether I looked back on this milestone with joy or regret. *What if I don't make it to forty-one?* I thought. *How would I want to be remembered then?*

> I sat down with my journal and began to write.

The answer excluded any mention of my coveted Model S. Did I want to be remembered for my dope ride? No, I want to be remembered for my character. I wanted to be remembered as a generous, caring, loving person who impacted the people and the world around me. It wasn't that I was unworthy of a Tesla— it's that there was something more worthy of the legacy I wished to leave.

Cultivating Generosity

Who do you picture when you hear the word philanthropist? You might envision a person with great wealth, giving generously because they have more than they can spend. You're probably thinking of a corporate executive in a plush office, not someone who shares half their burger with the beggar on the street despite being unable to afford groceries. Or the child waiting patiently to open the door for the elderly person approaching the entrance of the grocery store.

The word "philanthropy" comes from the late Latin *philanthropia*, meaning "kindliness, humanity, benevolence, and love to mankind." Notice something? The definition doesn't include wealth as a prerequisite. In fact, it doesn't even mention money.

Generosity is a mindset independent of financial well-being. John Rockefeller explained it this way: "I never would have been able to tithe the first million dollars I ever made if I had not tithed my first salary, which was $1.50 per week." If we keep our fists tight on what little bit we begin with, we will keep a death grip on our money when we have plenty.

> Generosity is a mindset independent of financial wellbeing.

One of the saddest things I see is when people withhold and delay generosity, and in so doing miss out on discovering all they had to gain in giving. They tell themselves, *If I were rich, I'd throw my money at the people and causes I care about.*

Okay, great—do you have five dollars that you could donate now? Do you have a minute to spare for the person who needs someone to talk to? A smile to the person passing on the street? You don't have to wait until you can give lavishly to experience the joy of giving.

There's an epidemic of mistrust in the world today that few are talking about. At its core is an absence of faith—the faith that things will work out by doing and being our best, by being generous with our gifts. We lack faith in ourselves, in others, and in the benevolence of a higher power, be it God or the Universe. So we hoard our kindness and money for lack of trust. That's the ultimate self-deception—withholding your own goodness and at the same time doubting the goodness of the world to which we belong. We question whether we'll be cared for if we take big risks in service of grand ambitions. And yet, we perpetuate the cycle by withholding the very care we're afraid we won't receive from the other.

Generosity is spiritual energy. Through giving, we don't just change the lives of those around us—we transform our own, creating a legacy of generosity that transcends material wealth and nurtures the soul. We become the kindness, humanity, benevolence, and love that we want for the world.

So, step forward, with an open heart and open hands, ready to plant seeds of generosity wherever you go. In the act of giving, you receive the greatest gift of all: a life rich in purpose, connection, and joy, echoing the timeless truth that in giving, we find the essence of living a truly dope life.

Generosity is spiritual energy.

40K for 40

When it comes to my giving, I will be transparent about my lack of transparency—I prefer not to talk about it.

I think that seeking credit for our giving robs us of its transformative power. I'll temporarily suspend that policy, though, for the purpose of this chapter and your benefit. Straight up—I hope to inspire you to embrace the act of giving and to discover the joy and abundance that flow from it.

You might have guessed by now that I didn't drive a Model S off the lot for my fortieth birthday. And you might've also guessed that such a decision didn't come without an epic duel between my ego and heart.

At first, I thought, *Let's give the money for the Tesla away.* Then, the voice of "reason" spoke. *Sarah wants to pull the trigger on buying your dream car, and you want to give the money away? Have you lost your mind?! This may never happen again!*

Obviously, I still had some work to do, so I kept writing and picking apart my motive. Maybe giving all the money away was just as self-indulgent as buying a Model S. Something was still off. Neither option felt right. Eventually, I got it—this was about legacy.

My original idea to give the money away was noble enough—it was also shortsighted. I'd donate the money, and that would be that—the impact would end there, with me.

I had a better idea. What if I provided an opportunity for people to participate in something bigger than themselves? I could make my donation, and then invite others to follow suit. I was aware of the common gap between ability and willingness to give. At the same time, I felt optimistic that my fortieth birthday would motivate those around me. And it would give them an opportunity to see that even donating one dollar starts to cultivate generosity...

In the end, I donated forty-thousand bucks, and together we gave over $83,000. While I didn't get a thank-you note from the Tesla dealership, I felt a lifetime of thank-yous for our work.

With the money we raised, we built a well for a community in Africa through a non-profit called Charity:Water, providing lifelong access to clean water for 735 individuals.

We also supported efforts to cure childhood cancer with donations to St. Jude, funded college education for four Haitian teenagers through Restore Haiti, and contributed to healing a racially divided world through the ministries led by my OG mentor and friend, Elwood Jones.

Then we made the dreams of four critically ill children come true through the Make-a-Wish Foundation.

I was driving a 2007 Toyota Corolla at this time, a reliable car if not the sexiest one on the road. At the same time, my family was in good health and had consistent access to clean running water and public schooling. By forgoing my dreams of a Model S, I seized the chance to extend these comforts to those who didn't win the cosmic lottery of being born in the modern Western world or the privilege of celebrating their fortieth birthday. This gift also deepened my appreciation of how truly blessed we are.

I had to lay my pride aside when my heart spoke up, trusting that there was a grander plan for me if I listened. Don't get me wrong—I placed my dream firmly on the back burner, hopeful I would one day find myself in the driver's seat of a Tesla. Nevertheless, I told myself, *If I never get that Tesla because I gave that money away, I will die a happy, fulfilled, and truly rich man.*

> I had to lay my pride aside when my heart spoke up.

That's why I decided to do what I did. If somehow I didn't make it to forty-one, then one of my friends would inherit the joy of giving and touching lives. And maybe they'd pass that legacy onto another person—a friend, a child, a perfect stranger.

Since the fundraising of my fortieth, I've had a half-dozen people who contributed tell me that they decided to do the same for their birthday. Why? Well, of course, to make a difference for others. And also because of the change giving had initiated in them. They'd seen their generosity truly and permanently impact the lives of others who were far less fortunate.

As I reflect on the most enriching experiences of my life, a few common threads spring to mind. Fun experiences and adventures around the world with my family. Wild nights with friends and loved ones who've passed on. Triumphs won by persevering against adversity to achieve something meaningful in my life. And one final thread that is woven into a dope life of true fulfillment: giving.

Open Hands, Full Soul

Spoiler alert: in the end, I got my Tesla. In fact, it was just over a year past my fortieth that I found it for a deal so low that it felt like a wink from the Big Guy in the sky. It was the car God set aside for me, and I love that car. Honestly, it's everything I dreamed it would be.

When I'm behind the wheel, do you think I second-guess the detour I took to invest in the lives of strangers and the hearts of people I love? I bet you know the answer to that.

> *The world changes one act of kindness at a time, and it starts with you.*

The journey was about more than just owning a dream car—it was a catalyst for a deeper realization. It symbolized the power of dreams and the beauty of aspiration. And in choosing to delay that dream for the sake of generosity, I discovered a more profound truth: the greatest impact we can make is through our acts of giving.

Imagine the ripple effect if we all embraced this spirit of giving. The world changes one act of kindness at a time, and it starts with you.

Loosening your grip on what's "yours" can feel scary. In fact, it can be downright scary. Yet, the beauty unfolds when we realize that the hand opened to give is also open to receive the richness of life.

To give from a place of abundance is one of the greatest experiences in life. It's sacred selfishness—giving with the knowledge of what

> *Everything worth doing in life requires trust.*

it does for and in *you*. It's a nudge from your heart toward what you're capable of, the courage to get out of your comfort zone and give something away, to trust life, to trust God, to trust yourself.

And everything worth doing in life requires trust—taking on a job that involves great challenges and great opportunities, starting a business, making the journey from couch to 5K, jumping from an airplane. Accomplishment brings joy. Why? Because it's a triumph over the disease we can all relate to: doubt that we're enough. Accomplishment is evidence of what happens when we trust in our ability to grow and overcome the rigidity of our present limitations.

Remember, succumbing to worry and negativity becomes a self-fulfilling prophecy and creates the quality of life you fear. When you ruminate about things going wrong, challenges serve as evidence that what you feared is happening. You're not sure your business idea will succeed, so you abandon it when others don't respond with enthusiasm right away. The burning in your legs is proof you aren't up to the task of running that 5k, not evidence that you're expanding your limits. So just as you feared, your business fails, and you never finish the race.

Feedback isn't taken as a gift and an opportunity to move toward competence, but as evidence of incompetence. So you cower. You fail in the only way you can stomach. By withholding your participation. By withholding your gifts. The result? You end up stuck with the very lifestyle you feared you'd live.

I don't want you to have that quality of life. I want you to embrace an abundance of spirit first, with abundance in all aspects of your life following. I want you to breathe, enjoy, and trust in the growth that magically happens when you push yourself. That is the generous life, one that grows from the inside out. That's the life where you remain open to give and receive freely.

If more people trusted enough to put themselves out there, they'd discover that what you give comes back multiplied—not because you give to get, but because you grow into a stronger person by giving.

When money takes on that cyclical nature—coming, going, coming, going—we're growing ourselves.

MAKING LIFE DOPE:

So, as you journey toward your own aspirations, I urge you to remember the paradoxical power of getting through giving. Perhaps that means rethinking a long-held dream or re-prioritizing your goals. Whatever you do, the rewards of such acts extend far beyond the immediate. Through giving, we enrich not just the lives of those we touch but also our own. And these ways are more profound than any material possession. That's the cycle of generosity. We fill our hearts by emptying our hands, discovering that true fulfillment comes through what we give, not what we gain.

> True fulfillment comes through what we give, not what we gain.

Now grab your Life Is Dope journal or workbook and respond to the following:

- How would you describe your relationship with money?
    - Are you afraid of losing it? In love with getting more of it? Too good for it? Ashamed of having it? Something else?
- What's your earliest memory of engaging in this way with money?
    - How has this relationship impacted you in fulfilling the dreams and desires in your heart? (Hint: get real real REAL honest with yourself)
- Have you ever had a dream to help a cause in a big way?
    - If so, what is it?
    - If you haven't accomplished this, how has your relationship to money and giving impacted you in reaching this goal?
- What are some non-money areas you can give?

- Sometimes if we don't have 100% of what we want to give, we don't give anything. Often because of feeling shame and believing "it's not enough to make a difference."
- To break this destructive cycle, I want you to choose a charity, person, or cause you can give a minimum of five dollars to right now! (like right now, right now)
- If you don't know where to give, scan the QR code and choose one of the charities.
- When you give, I want you to do away with the old "it's not enough" thinking. Celebrate and behave like you gave five million dollars! You just helped change someone's life!!!
- Take sixty seconds to journal about how doing this feels. Reflect on how life would look differently if you celebrated what you DO do, rather than "shoulding on yourself" for not doing "enough."

BONUS:

Make life simple. Download the official Life Is Dope Accompaniment workbook for free by visiting MichaelAnthonyTV.com/LifeIsDope or scanning this QR code. If you already did, tag me on social @MichaelAnthonyTV so we can virtually dab it out.

STORY 14

Opportunities Come With an Expiration Date

> *This is the moment*
> *Tonight is the night, we'll fight 'til it's over*
> *So we put our hands up, like the ceiling can't hold us*
> —**Macklemore, "Can't Hold Us"**

In 2012, between getting the speakers bureau up and running and going to school full time, I had my hands full. On one side of the coin, my schedule put me at a disadvantage relative to my classmates. On the other side, I was light years ahead of nearly everyone in both life experience and professional resources.

This was never more true than when we were tasked to write a paper about the companies of the future. While others scrambled to find an angle and resources they could use to make a valid point, I lined up an interview with a business associate who was shaping the future of commerce.

A few years prior, Jared founded a web-based home improvement business that challenged the industry's brick-and-mortar titans. His innovation proved so disruptive and threatening to the market share of the established players that his company was eventually acquired—for over $100 million.

Leading up to our interview, I felt relatively settled in my professional path. I was starting a company within the company, doing everything I could to make it a success. At the same time, I wanted to do more and earn more. Going back to school was just one of the steps I was taking to make it happen.

When the day came for our interview, I pulled together the questions I'd prepared and sat down to make the call from my "office." I use the term loosely because it was actually the corner of my bedroom with a desk salvaged from my neighbor's trash and an out-of-date computer gifted to me by an old coworker.

As the call started, aside from the fact that his office was likely more than a few feet from his bed, I was immediately struck by the differences between us. Obviously, he had achieved more significant professional success and in all likelihood had more extravagant belongings. However, the most glaring difference I sensed between us was in our disposition. What I admired most about him weren't tangible assets, but the qualities he exuded: joy, purpose, focus, and freedom.

The middle class is an experiment.

He answered my call from the sideline of his kid's soccer game. Here was this guy who'd delivered the kind of results most only dream of, and he was carrying himself like he didn't have a care in the world. He was calm, grounded, and friendly, with seemingly no use for pretense. I liked him, and it wasn't long before getting the information for my paper took a backseat to understand what made him tick.

Jumping from my carefully prepared script, I asked him a question I was genuinely curious about, hoping to glean some principles to apply to my own journey. "What motivated you to build this company?"

"I've seen a larger gap grow between the wealthy and the poor than I could have imagined in my lifetime. You know," he said, pausing thoughtfully before continuing, "the middle class is an experiment."

Wrecked

Most Americans count on the persistence of the middle class as a reliable path to stability. It's the bedrock of the American Dream—a good, honest living leading to a hard-earned, blissed-out retirement.

Hell, at the time he said that I was relying on it too, but not just as a socioeconomic label. I was living as if time were endless. I told myself it was okay to move at a snail's pace because my kids would have the same opportunities to advance as I did. I had focus. I had vision. But I lacked urgency.

I was acting as if I was going to live to be 500 years old, disconnected from the reality that life could change abruptly. Little did I know, that a conversation intended to help me write a paper would completely wreck my worldview. In the best possible way.

> The middle class as we know it is dying.

Shaken by his claim that the herd I was struggling to join was scattering, I decided to do my own research. Maybe, I reasoned, he was just throwing this out willy-nilly as someone who'd already made it. If he was wrong, what did he have to lose?

So I took a deep dive down a rabbit hole, researching everything I could find about the state of the middle class. And well, I'll save you the twists and turns, the rationalizations, and "Yes, buts." All you need to know is what I found only deepened my agitation.

And things have only gotten worse since I did my first round of research: there's clear evidence of a steady decline in the middle class over the last fifty years. Steady, that is, until Covid came along—then the gap between the rich and the poor flew wide open.

LIFE IS DOPE

Between 2020 and 2021, more than a hundred million people fell below the poverty line at the same time that billionaires increased their wealth by $4.4 trillion. People are headed toward one or the other extreme, not closer to the middle. What he said was absolutely correct: the middle class as we know it is dying.

I'm no history buff—I was studying business to become a better businessman. What I learned, though, convinced me that the trajectory of the successful businessperson of tomorrow will bear little resemblance to those of yesterday. The middle class, I learned, was a product of the Industrial Revolution. In other words, it's only existed for about 150 years. It's an experiment, one I'd been unknowingly participating in for my entire life leading up to our call.

Don't get me wrong. When I look to the future, I don't see all doom and gloom. Though the middle class as we know it may be changing, I believe that innovation and new policies may provide a level of comfort and security beyond what kings enjoyed 200 years ago, even if traditional paths to upward mobility are shifting.

> When I look to the future, I don't see all doom and gloom.

Nevertheless, I intend to anticipate the best and plan for the worst. All along, my thought had been, *Just keep nudging forward bit by bit. That's all that really matters. Eventually, you'll find success and stability.*

In other words, I was taking my time, believing I'd eventually land that well-paying job that would carry me to a comfortable retirement. That self-justifying rationalization was challenged by my interviewee's claim and dismantled completely by my investigation that followed. It was a Red Pill-Blue Pill moment: I could continue to live in a state of blissful ignorance to the impending end of the American Dream as we know it or wake up to the dawn of a new reality.

A Legacy at Stake

This all may be very disruptive to your outlook and everyday life, just as it was to mine. Honestly, I didn't like the idea of my kids not having the safety net of the middle class. The thought felt very dystopian. It still does. Remember, though: that doesn't make it *not* true.

Certainly, there was a part of me that wanted to carry on as though the conversation hadn't happened. In fact, the dawning reality left me feeling like complete shit. I went from perceiving myself as sensible and hopeful to complacent and lazy. I'd been pursuing the good enough life, counting on the American Dream to pick up the slack and make it great. I lost my ignorance, and my bliss along with it.

I knew it was on me to come to terms with this information and follow this guy's example by getting out ahead of it. Remember, the same state of affairs I perceived as a dire threat to my future served as his driving force to building a company worth a fortune—one that would change the lives of his children and his children's children.

And he wasn't some arrogant, shady character. He had a lifestyle, results, *and* character I wanted to emulate. So I laid aside all of the ego I'd invested into this dream of middle-class bliss. Better yet, I put aside the safety net that kept me from dreaming beyond the bounds of my ego. My mindset transformed from a passive "It would be nice to be rich, but at least I can be part of the middle class" to an active "I can't wait around for things to happen—I must take action."

There were two kids down the hall depending on their dad to guide them in life. I saw that I had the chance to usher in the new way, to bridge the gap between the middle class and wealth, instead of pointing them toward an old rickety bridge held up with fraying ropes.

But what would I say to my kids? Would I show them that they should pursue comfort over ambition? Would their memories of me be peppered with countless nights of mediocre results? Would they wax nostalgic about all the scrolling through social media I did? Or would they remember how Dad doubled down on himself and his family and went for it?

My conversation with this entrepreneur happened over a decade ago. And I don't see things getting better, do you? The model of upward mobility through toeing the line is fading away and will likely be a distant memory by the time kids of this generation reach adulthood. And yet, paradoxically, there are opportunities available today that were unheard of for decades.

As we discussed in Chapter 12, many of the financial and logistical obstacles to developing high-income skills in the past no longer exist. However, the complacent won't be the ones to reap these benefits. While some are still caught up in the dream, those who are waking up and embracing the new reality will get ahead.

> The complacent won't be the ones to reap these benefits.

So this is my current mantra: it's never been easier than it is today. And at the same time, I work like the worst about tomorrow is true. I behave under the assumption that the opportunities won't last.

Why? Here's how I'll answer any naysayer about the notion that the middle class is fading. Let's say the trends of the last fifty years reverse, and the middle class experiences a boom.

I sincerely hope this is the case. I hope the middle class not only survives but thrives because its stability is crucial for so many. Yet, hope is not a strategy. It's about confronting reality as it is, reading the data, and recognizing that no cavalry is coming to save you.

> I hope the middle class not only survives but thrives.

Individual success is up to you so make the most of each situation and seize every opportunity that comes your way! If the middle class undergoes a revival, will you regret working your ass off as if every second and every opportunity might be your last? There's always something you can be doing today to better yourself and your position relative to where you'd like to be.

Ultimately, opportunities arise at the intersection of the past and present. They're built upon the sacrifices of those who came generations before us. In the same way, our children's futures depend on us. So what if this ends up being the last generation of upward mobility? Sure, you can justify all the reasons you didn't capitalize. Of course, that's the very attitude that will ensure you see all the risks and completely miss the opportunities—you get what you look for.

If that's you, yank your head out of that narrow, musty space you've buried it in and get a whiff of the vast, vibrant world outside. Your legacy is at stake!

Living Into Your Legacy

Yes, the middle class is dying—the rich are getting richer and the poor are getting poorer. That's the bad news. Or is it? For those who aren't looking to the herd for answers, the landscape is ripe with opportunity. In a world where the narrative often paints the wealthy as villains, it's crucial to be honest with ourselves about our intentions and aspirations.

> Your legacy is at stake!

I've been the dishwasher, worked in retail, and earned less than minimum wage at nonprofits. I also know what it's like to be a successful, financially independent business owner. That transition was not always smooth, and as you've been reading, it certainly wasn't easy. I can tell you, though, that it is far more taxing to the spirit to stay the same than it is to do the work of forging ahead.

And in this forging, I literally had to wrestle with whether I had the conviction to be a Gandhi-like figure and work to disrupt the whole global system. Eventually, I concluded that I did not. While I admire such conviction, the truth is that my goals are more personal—

enjoying the journey, creating the best opportunities for my kids, and leaving the world a better place. For all.

At the end of the day, I believe life is about making the most of what we innately have. It's about exercising our gifts. That's why they're called "gifts," by the way, because they're meant to be given.

Today, I'm using and giving my gifts, not waiting around for someone to give me one. I've gradually chipped away at the "woe-is-me" bullshit, choosing instead to get after it. No, not through grand acts of defiance or societal upheaval, but in the everyday choices that add up to a meaningful difference.

MAKING LIFE DOPE:

Here are some prompts to help you take control and make a difference in your own life right now. Grab your Life Is Dope journal or workbook and reflect on the following:

- A GPS only works when it knows where it's starting from. Accepting your current situation is the first step toward change. Being brutally honest —and kind—with yourself, write out where you believe you are on your journey.

  > *A GPS only works when it knows where it's starting from.*

  - What does the final destination look like for you?
- Take a moment to reflect on success and what it means to you. If no one was judging you, what would bring you the most joy and sense of accomplishment in life?
  - Being a parent who has kids who love and admire you? Being a badass CEO? Or being a stay-at-home spouse who lights up his partner's world? (The only wrong answer isn't honest.)
- What is ONE thing you're good at that others appreciate?

- Making people smile? Seeing situations without drama? Being caring and compassionate? Being honest, even when it hurts someone's ego?
- How could you use your "gift" to intentionally bring dopeness to others lives starting today?
- What are 1-2 areas where playing the victim has been holding you back from making your life dope?
  - What is one simple action you can take (now) to re-take your power and live the dope life?
- Legacy matters more than we think. take a few moments to write down how you want to be remembered.
  - What impact do you want to leave on the world and next generations?
  - Do you want to be the first human on Mars? Do you want to be the "cool aunt" who helps shape an amazing human? Maybe you want to donate $10,000 to your favorite charity?
  - Now, take a few more moments to allow your heart to dream and write down what it says.

> *The way I see it, you can get upset about the way things "should be" and shout into the wind about all that you're owed, or you can actively seek prosperity and use what you have to make the world a more beautiful place.*

Ultimately, the dilemma's the same for all of us: what are you gonna do with your life? Do you want to go out like a victim, grumbling to the nurse about how the game was rigged and run by a bunch of crooks while he nods, half-listening—"There there, Mr. Anthony, get some rest?" Or are you going to take fucking ownership of your life and decide where you can make an actual difference *in spite of* the rigged game?

Here's the truth as I see it: I like the idea of making a shit ton of money and all of the compounding influence that comes along with it. I want to have the money to fund people who desire to disrupt this world for good. The way I see it, you can get upset about the way things "should be" and shout into the wind about all that you're owed, or you can actively seek prosperity and use what you have to make the world a more beautiful place.

The fact is, no set of circumstances, no matter how limiting, can prevent you from taking control of your own growth. So choose your target, embrace the journey, and understand that growth and success are processes, not destinations. Every step forward is one closer to a doper life.

> *Every step forward is one closer to a doper life.*

BONUS:

Take action before the book is over. Dive deeper by using the official Life Is Dope Accompaniment workbook for free, by visiting MichaelAnthonyTV.com/LifeIsDope or scanning this QR code. For those making their life dope, I love getting dope updates on social @michaelanthonytv

STORY 15

I'm Not Broken, I'm a Prism

Life is not always a comfortable ride
Everybody's got scars that they hide
And everybody plays the fool sometimes, yeah
Just be as you are
—**Mike Posner, "Be As You Are"**

Jeremy Cowart has photographed a who's who of A-list celebrities: Taylor Swift, Spike Lee, the Kardashians, Gwyneth Paltrow, Emma Stone, Gary Vee—the list goes on.

He's also photographed me.

Though his work is known the world over, Jeremy's studio is right around the corner from my house in Franklin, Tennessee. I knew his work, and it spoke to me in much the same way as the Tesla does. It embodies a one-of-a-kind beauty made possible by seemingly impossible means.

> I was privileged to step into Jeremy's world and witness his creativity in action.

During our photoshoot, I was privileged to step into Jeremy's world and witness his creativity in action. With a mix of meticulousness and spontaneity, he places prisms over the camera lens, manipulating light to create striking and unconventional images. By playing with light refraction in that way, he alters what we might deem a "normal" view of life through the lens into a truly extraordinary view of the subject.

Jeremy's photography is not always "pretty," at least not in the conventional sense. And yet, it's never bland or uninspired. Where other photographers pursue pristine composition, sharp lines, and harmonious color schemes, he seeks the beautiful chaos of life. Jagged edges, blurred lines, colorful disarray—all these elements coalesce into his signature style, an unapologetic embrace of imperfection.

That's Jeremy Cowart's magic: taking the ordinary and elevating it into the magnificent. It's a vision I was privileged to witness and one that would come to impact the way I viewed my place in the world.

> *Where other photographers pursue pristine composition, sharp lines, and harmonious color schemes, he seeks the beautiful chaos of life.*

Broken

Throughout the journey of writing this book, my family and business have flourished. And yet, despite all that, I continued to grow through the mental and emotional scars of my childhood and young adulthood.

Doubts crept in: *Nobody knows how to fix me*, the story goes. *I'm not just beyond repair, I'm inherently defective.*

I've tried just about every brand of therapy known to man. Some have helped, but none have brought me to the level of inner peace I desired. Sure, they've brought hordes of monsters out from under my bed where I could face them. But as I was working to bring my story to you, some of the boldest and most tenacious among them continued to kick my ass in broad daylight.

Well, there was just one kind of therapy I hadn't tried, one I'd heard sometimes works when nothing else does: eye movement desensitization and reprocessing therapy, or EMDR. And by this point, I was up for anything.

One of my long-time coaches reacted to my intention with skepticism. "Mike," she said, "my concern is that by doing this EMDR therapy, you're adopting the energy that you're broken and need to be fixed."

Her words, though well-intentioned, went in one ear and out the other. She didn't get it. How could she? She only knew the version of me that I presented to the world, the one where I painstakingly held all my pieces together. Beneath that facade, she was blind to the real me—the me I harshly judged and often despised.

And while I understand what she meant now, I was in no state to make any sense of what she was saying at the time. To her, I might have seemed just shy of normal, but inside, I felt beyond redemption—beyond the reach of simple fixes or societal acceptance. In my eyes, I was a lost cause.

> In my eyes, I was a lost cause.

I'd done all the work assigned to me, and jumped through every hoop, and I *still* felt broken, worn to the bone by the shame that had haunted me for longer than I could remember. This was my last-ditch effort. I had one, desperate desire: *just fix the pain.*

Emergency Intervention

I found myself in the midst of an unusual therapy session, the last in a series of five-hour "intensive" EMDR sessions. To me, this was a make-or-break experience, an intensive care emergency surgery for my mental well-being

Like the two sessions before, my therapist instructed me to close my eyes and hold a little vibrating paddle in each hand. The paddles vibrated back and forth at an even pace—left hand, right hand, left hand, right hand, back and forth. This led to activation in both sides of my brain, said the therapist, facilitating the processing and integration of traumatic memories.

My job was to simply hold my focus on some traumatic memory or related negative belief for a fixed duration, perhaps ninety seconds, and then note the sights, sounds, and smells that emerged as my mind wandered along its stream of consciousness.

Clutching these buzzing paddles initiated the same old laundry list of self-defeating questions that seemed to ask themselves: *Why am I not normal? Why is life so difficult? Why can't I just be like everyone else?*

This was my M.O. I just wanted to be normal, and yet, I felt doomed to remain hyper-aware of the fact that I never quite fit. Yeah, people liked being around me, but I was still haunted by the suspicion that their affection was insincere. I couldn't shake the feeling that if they really knew *all* of me, including the dark, shadow side, they'd disown me.

And I'm not talking about serial killer dark. I mean things like having a hot temper, being condescending, or overly critical. Add to that a strong sex drive, which, given my suppressive sexual upbringing, led to intense feelings of shame, guilt, and anger. These are the aspects I feared would alienate me from others, parts of myself that, if I'm honest, I am still working to understand, love, and accept.

Then, in the midst of this familiar turmoil, a vivid mental image appeared: I was in a big mountain home, gazing through a massive, spotless pane of glass overlooking a breathtaking mountain peak, flanked by sweeping valleys on either side.

At that moment, I recalled Jay, a mentor I had during my time at the financial education organization.

Jay was the embodiment of what I deemed "normal." He exuded the image of a family man, a model husband, and a loving, present dad. His demeanor remained consistently cool and steady, poised yet never stiff. He possessed a refined sense of humor, never seeking the spotlight but never shying away from it either. He used language in the ways we're all supposed to, swearing only at the most appropriate times—a restraint I admired.

More than anything, he carried an air of confidence, peace of mind, and apparent freedom from life's challenges that I desperately yearned to experience. Just like the image in my mind's eye, he was, to me, like a large panoramic window, crystal clear—free from muck, grime, cracks, or dings—revealing the most unmarred perspective of reality possible.

It's important to remember, though, that just because someone like Jay appears flawless, it doesn't mean they are without imperfections. They may be very good at managing them. Or maybe their poise and resilience were hard-earned and worthy of aspiring to. Regardless, it's important to remember that the seeming perfection of the "clear pane windows" of the world doesn't make them more valuable. Each of us, from the Jay to the misfits, the pristine or smudged, contributes uniquely to the diversity of human experience.

I could've used that perspective back then because, as soon as that vision appeared, the self-judgment followed, my former mentor's apparent normalcy serving as an indictment on everything that was off about me. *That's not me,* I insisted. *I'm not a spotless pane of glass. I'm a broken, filthy pane of glass.* But then, as I began to choke on my shame, something else took hold.

I recalled my photoshoot with Jeremy Cowart. I saw myself strolling down the pavement in a crowd of anonymous people. Except the "me" I saw looked like a fifteen-sided cylindrical glass prism, cracked, with pieces missing around my head. The sunlight streamed down on me and passed through, casting vibrant colors onto the faces and paths of passersby—reds of passion, blues of calm, greens of growth. The light, like divine energy passing through its conduit, brought healing, peace, joy, and happiness to those it touched.

In this moment, I understood that despite, or perhaps because of, my imperfections, I was a vessel for something greater. This revelation reshaped how I saw myself and my role in the world. Like a prism, I was channeling what was universal and sacred, impacting those around me in profound and positive ways. It was strikingly clear that my unique qualities, what I'd viewed as distortions and brokenness, were a source of grace and healing for those around me. At that moment, a realization struck me:

I'm not broken. I'm a prism.

Perfectly Imperfect

When the session ended, it felt as though a tectonic shift had occurred in my mind, evaporating old barriers and unleashing a free flow of new thoughts and emotional insights. Suddenly, I started to understand the unique perspective I bring to the world.

> *I'm not broken.*
> *I'm a prism.*

Unlike those who rigidly defend their version of "normal," I welcome and celebrate perspectives different from my own. I don't always agree. I don't always understand. It might even make me uncomfortable. And I have a deep well of compassion for others—a well I realized I had seldom allowed myself to drink from. I deprived myself of the grace and understanding that I so naturally extended to others.

I thought of one of my favorite artists, Prince, who by any societal standards would be considered a weirdo. His childhood wasn't all diamonds and pearls. His parents separated when he was two. He struggled with epilepsy, which led to seizures, sometimes in the middle of class. He was pitied by some, and bullied by others. Had you encountered him on the street, you may well have dismissed him as a nutjob.

And that was his genius. Despite it all, he never sought normalcy. Instead, he reveled in his uniqueness, saying, "A strong spirit transcends rules." Prince's legacy, like a beam of purple light refracting through a prism, was his ability to transform adversity into art.

Reflecting on this, I recognized my own battle against the quirks and scars that define me. Whether born from trauma or inherent traits, these aspects of my personality refract life's light uniquely, creating patterns no "normal" lens could. It's in this realization that I found freedom—not in erasing these parts, but in celebrating them for the complexity and depth they add to my existence.

> *It's in this realization that I found freedom.*

This journey isn't mine alone—it's a path we all tread. Maybe you've faced hurdles like abuse, felt ostracized for your appearance or speech, or live through the challenges of a physical disability. These aren't mere details—they are profound aspects of your story that have contributed to who you are. Whether your nature is innate or shaped by experiences, it is what makes you uniquely "you." You can lament that you lost the genetic lottery. You can focus on the ways that you were wronged.

> *The only force powerful enough to bring these shadows into the light—transforming them with understanding and healing—is love.*

Or, what if you embrace your uniqueness, truly owned your prism, and let the light shine through you? What if you gazed at how the light distorts, breaks into colors, and dances with your quirks and features with openness and curiosity, perhaps even playfulness?

Imagine appreciating the rich tapestry of your life experiences—both joyful and painful—that forged you into the person you are today.

Our society's narrow focus on fitting in overlooks the beauty in our collective oddities and imperfections. All too often, we strive to conceal what truly makes us stand out, neglecting the very qualities that require our acceptance and love. We try to suppress or ignore the sources of our shame, hoping they'll simply disappear. Yet, the only force powerful enough to bring these shadows into the light—transforming them with understanding and healing—is love.

Own Your Weird

We've all experienced hardships we didn't invite and definitely didn't cause. Somewhere along the line, something got knocked around. The prism got cracked and the light refracted. You were cruising down the highway on a clear, sunny day—or maybe your parents or your parents' parents were—and a pebble flew up, and nicked the window. As a result, the light got bent and distorted. It rendered some part of you a little… different.

As you've discovered by now, I've had my fair share of nicks over the years, and I'm quirky as hell. I attempted to hide them for a long time—from myself just as much as from others. I put "normal" on a pedestal, worshiping and craving it. Eventually, though, I learned there's a huge price to guarding yourself for the sake of appearing normal.

Too often, we're quick to judge the "unusual" characteristics that reflect our individual nature and unique experiences. Maybe you're a man who feels better in women's clothing. If Harry Styles can rock a dress, then so can you. Maybe you're one of the many customers who contribute to the staggering half-million dollars a month in revenue that my friend's friend makes by farting into jars and selling them—you can't make this shit up.

Or maybe you're like me, a man who has come to embrace his quirky sense of fashion, one who has realized that attraction to women and handbags can coexist. And holy fuck, do I love handbags. Or perhaps you feel like dancing even though everyone else is sitting. I remember being on a cruise, in the pool, watching a few concerts. There I was, cheering, clapping, and singing like I was part of the band. I felt weird and out of place, yet I was just being genuine, not seeking attention. Interestingly, over the next few days, several people came up to me separately, thanking me for having fun during the concerts. They told me it helped them loosen up and enjoy themselves more.

The point is, it's time we broaden our perspective on what we consider "normal," for ourselves and our fellow man, woman, or whatever falls in between. If people are dropping a fat chunk of their paychecks to smell jarred farts, then probably, many of us have a sense of abnormality that's a hell of a lot more normal than we think.

I don't feel defective anymore, like a fuck-up that needs to be unfucked. I resolve to embrace my quirks with grace, not just to myself but to the world around me. Maybe that opens me to misunderstandings and judgments. But those who love me, in all of my eccentricity, truly love me—the real me. And until we learn to be 100% ourselves, and to be loved for that authentic person, we'll live in captivity. I'm still a work in process. I'm learning to let down my shackles of shame, and learning that the more I do, the more rewarding my life becomes—that's what "making life dope" is all about.

> I don't feel defective anymore.

In fact, embracing my own brokenness has deepened my gift of empathy for others. I know how to roll with a damaging blow. I know how to coach people through downturns in their business and their personal lives because I've had the gift of rolling with so many punches on the road to where I am today. I've learned how to make beauty from pain. That's precisely why I preach it: because I want you to find that you're capable of making your life dope in the same way.

My Life is Dope

I made a shirt that says "My life is dope." The point is not that every second of every day is dope. It's not some boast about "living my best life." It's what I declare, and the declaration I wish for others to adopt—a resolution, if you will.

When you say, "My life is dope," it means that no matter what has or will happen to you in life, you will flip the coin. You'll choose to believe life is happening *for* you, not to you. You are being polished, not punished. You were born for more, and there is always another side to the storm. And you can get there, with joy and gratitude.

If you're like me, you've taken some knocks. You've lived through a lot of hard experiences. Maybe you're not "normal," and honestly, that's okay. Imagine a world where everyone was the same. It might be stable, but it would lack the vibrancy of life itself.

> *You're a prism, a perfectly imperfect masterpiece.*

You're a prism, a perfectly imperfect masterpiece, reflecting the light of the world in a way that not a single person on earth could do in the same way. Each of us, whether conventional or unusual, plays a unique part in the kaleidoscope of human experience.

MAKING LIFE DOPE:

Here's what I've learned and what I wish for you to embrace in your journey. So grab your Life Is Dope journal or workbook and reflect on these final questions:

- Where are you not allowing your genuine self to shine?
    - How would your life and others lives be positively impacted if you allowed your true self to shine through?
- What areas do you feel judged by others?
    - Where are you afraid to show your quirks and scars?
    - What if your idiosyncrasies and scars are not just to be accepted; they're to be embraced as markers of your unique journey and teachers of deep love?
- Spend a few moments writing about how you feel right now.
    - Are you afraid?
    - Are you overcome with peace?
    - Is there anger or shame?
    - Why do you think these emotions are here?
    - What could you do right now to turn unbeneficial feelings into beneficial ones?
- How would life look and feel different if you fully embraced your uniqueness?

Facing your pain through methods like journaling, open communication, and therapy can be pivotal in unraveling self-judgment. Learning to love and accept your unique qualities is an act of ownership over your life and reality. By nurturing your roots, you learn to live confidently, extend compassion towards yourself, and offer grace to others who may judge.

Embracing your uniqueness is the ultimate act of self-love and ownership.

In a world that often seeks to dim the light of those who dare to shine, embracing your uniqueness is the ultimate act of self-love and ownership. Your reality, your dope life, is yours to create. It's a canvas awaiting the colors only your prism can cast.

So, cheers to you for loving yourself, in all of your quirks. Here's to living boldly, with grace and compassion. The world doesn't need more conformity. It needs more YOU, painting the world with the beauty of your unique existence. May you find the courage to keep your window pane spotless or let your light fracture into a thousand colors if it gets chipped, making the world a richer place with your genuine presence.

BONUS:

Take action right now or you may forget about the opportunity to make growth easy by downloading the official Life Is Dope Accompaniment workbook, music playlists and more- all for free. Visit MichaelAnthonyTV.com/LifeisDope or scanning this QR code. Inspire others by tagging me on social @MichaelAnthonyTV

CONCLUSION

What's Next

I'm the king of my own land
Facing tempests of dust, I'll fight until the end
Creatures of my dreams, raise up and dance with me
Now and forever
I'm your king
—M83, "Outro"

Nothing changes in a month. Some things change in a year. Everything changes in a decade.

Have you been seeking change for a while? Are you a month in? A year? Has the only consistency been your inconsistency? All this toil and no fruit to show for it. Maybe you've fallen short of your aspirations so often and for so long that you're beginning to question whether this is just who you are—a failure.

Life feels painful. You're adrift in a vast ocean with no land in sight, and your hope is waning. *Maybe,* you think, *the payoff will never come.*

> *Nothing changes in a month. Some things change in a year. Everything changes in a decade.*

This is when most throw in the towel, reasoning that if trying hard isn't working, then they might as well take it easy. And if striving for their dreams seems to be getting nowhere, they might as well settle.

However, a few recognize and eventually uncover the truth: progress takes its time. Progress waits to see that you're truly committed.

I was being buried, and sometimes burying myself, for nearly three decades. It wasn't until my late twenties that I started to dig myself out, even when it felt at times that the universe (or I) was throwing dirt back in. For the decade leading up to writing this book, I was laser-focused, my head down. I did a lifetime of work on myself across those ten years.

Now, I can say something I couldn't even fathom back then—I *love* who I am. I am content, not satisfied—I have not "arrived." Nevertheless, when I look in the mirror, I see someone deserving of success and all the love necessary to take it. I see a person becoming who he was all along, reclaiming the person he once lost in the chaos of life.

So why bother writing this book, sorting through my dirty laundry, and airing it out for the world to see? Because I know what it's like to wrestle with doubt and faith. I remember each of the crossroads where I almost gave up on myself and my dreams. I know how close I came to giving up on life, to robbing myself of the joy that comes with living well. I nearly missed out on the self-respect I experience today—the chance to look in the mirror and like the person looking back.

> *I love who I am.*

I'm here to urge you to keep going, to hold onto the worthiness of your dreams. Remember, belief is your secret weapon. Martin Luther King Jr. also urged us to believe when he said, "Faith is taking the first step even when you don't see the whole staircase." Let these words guide you, no matter how distant your goals seem.

Every one of us is inherently worthy. When I was staying in a Motel 6, I was worthy of the Ritz-Carlton Reserve. When I was driving a $500 Nissan, I was worthy of my dream car.

Let's be real—there were (and still are) times I doubted my worth. But my faith is stronger than my doubts. By acting on my belief, I eventually proved that my sense of worth had been right all along. Worthiness is a birthright—it's claimed through belief and action.

> My faith is stronger than my doubts.

You

So this brings me to the one person I wrote this book for: you.

Have you established a vision for your future based on asking yourself, every single day, that question that can sometimes be so uncomfortable: *Why am I here? Why am I doing what I am doing?*

Some people never ask those questions of themselves, and they reach the end of their lives burdened with regret. Why? Because they lost their urgency for the life that only happens once. Again and again, they were invited by their conscience to toe the line and run *their* race, and every time, they bought into their own bullshit, allowing doubts about their worthiness to paralyze them into inaction.

It's not practical. It's too hard. I don't have enough time. I have plenty of time left. I'm too young. I'm too old. I'm not strong enough/ smart enough/confident enough. All the while, they didn't do what works: commitment and consistent action. They were potential winners who chose failure by their failure to commit and to act.

In reality, there are only two ways to fail: refusing to start and refusing to learn when we give our all and don't (yet) succeed. Don't live in that in-between. That's the arid ground of stagnation and regret.

Will you also feel frustrated? Yes! And that's not only normal, it's also *good*. It's there to serve you, not hurt you. Lean into that frustration. It's the rocket fuel intended to propel you out of the slums and into orbit, where the gravity of doubt that once weighed you down gives way to the realization of your immense power. The frustration is there to tell you, "There is more."

The Present and the Possible

This book chronicles the lessons I unearthed through the day-to-day grind, in times when I didn't enjoy the benefit of hindsight to reassure me... *it's happening*. These stories show how I learned to make life dope by facing each day with courage and hope.

These are lessons I would've lost if I hadn't persevered in the direction pointed by *hope* — for another day that turned into a week, a week that became a month, then a year, then a decade.

It's not a comprehensive list. In fact, there will likely be additional lessons by the time the book goes to print, additional chapters I could add to the book of my life. So while they may not be exhaustive, they are universal.

> *Each obstacle tests whether the strength of your conviction can bear the weight of your vision.*

And yet, no matter how universally applicable a lesson may be, they are as good as useless if you don't practice them. The fifteen lessons shared in these pages are united by one fundamental principle that determines their impact on your life: ownership. What truly matters for you—and the reason I laid out my baggage for the world to see—is what you take from my story and write into yours.

And so, armed with faith you're meant for more and the grace to keep going when you bump up against your current limitations—start. Select a single concept from these pages that resonated with you and pursue it. Such an action, even if you feel it's "not enough," has the power to place you on a path to the dopest life you can envision.

All that matters—ever—is what you do now. Dwelling on past failures only feeds pessimistic projections about how you might fuck up in the future. Thinking about how far you have to go just undermines your only hope of getting there —taking the next step.

That's how your vision will become a reality—not just one-off action when the wind's at your back, but through consistent and sustained action, no matter the conditions. Every effort and victory, no matter how small, brings you one step closer to that horizon.

And are you going to fuck up? Of course! Your little arms and legs wobbled before you could crawl. You had to fall on your face time and again before you could walk. Falling short of your vision does not invalidate the vision itself— it's learning from your mistakes, the information you need to narrow the gap between the present and the possible. And on the way there, every challenge is an opportunity to prove to yourself what you're made of, preparing you for trials that once seemed impossible. Each obstacle tests whether the strength of your conviction can bear the weight of your vision.

Inflection Point

So as you reach the end of this book, don't just go on with life as usual. The world is filled with enough hurt and lost people with immense and unrealized potential. You need you. The world needs

> Grace—undeserved favor —is the essence from which love is woven.

your gifts. Don't let your journey stop here. Make it worth your while. Make it dope. Decide, now. Act, now.

And celebrate it! Celebrate you. Extend yourself *grace*.

You see, love is the most powerful force in the universe. And if love is the force that holds the universe together, then grace—undeserved favor —is the essence from which love is woven.

Yes, life can be excruciating. I've been there—through abuse, neglect, violence, and betrayal. And guess what? Every single one of those experiences shaped and served me in some way. I am here now.

How? By allowing grace into my life. When you embrace grace, you perceive life differently. You find the strength to let go of seeing life as a series of events happening "to you" and instead view it as a canvas of opportunities for transformation and growth. Remember, life is happening *for you*.

Simply being here, existing in this moment, is enough. *You are enough.* Your Creator, God, the Universe, Infinite Intelligence, whatever name you assign that higher power, placed you here for a reason—not to experience suffering, but to fulfill a unique purpose.

So let the person you see yourself becoming cheer you ahead. *You are worthy. You are worth it!* Go rescue that person you've been since the beginning before you got buried beneath the bullshit. Even when it's tough—especially when it's tough—*remember to lean into grace*.

When we do so, we learn to extend that grace outward, to fulfill our ultimate purpose—growing and sharing our gifts so we can better love those around us.

Remember This

As we approach our landing, I urge you to embrace this thought: you have one life, a life filled with potential and possibility. This is not a dress rehearsal. Lean into grace, let it guide you through the discomfort, and watch as it transforms both your life and the lives of those around you.

Nothing changes in a month. Some things change in a year. Everything changes in a decade.

Everything that you need is already within you. Now, go get it!

To Your Success,

Michael Anthony

@MichaelAnthonyTV

ACKNOWLEDGMENTS

I've spent as much, if not more time on this section than any other in the book... Because these are stories of my life, it's appropriate for me to acknowledge the thousands (literally) who have played a role in me becoming who I am. I've constructed lists upon lists... and inevitably, that list keeps coming up short.

So, rather than publish the 10 pages of triple-column names I've written, knowing I'm leaving someone genuinely near to my heart out, I'm taking a different approach.

IF you've played a part in me becoming who I am today- lent an ear or a smile, showed up when I needed, given me clothes or food, helped fix cars, mentored me, prayed for me, coached me, created something that's inspired me, taught me, loved me, shown me grace, shared a laugh, a late night or early morning. If you comment, like, support any of my social channels... please put your name below.

It would be my privilege to get a selfie with you one day of us both holding this book!

Thank you for helping me realize Life is Dope.

ENDNOTES

Story 1
1. Rory Callaghan, "Our 3 Brains—Why 95% of Our Behaviors Are Not Conscious (Extended Review)," rorycallaghan.com, 13 Dec 2021, https://www.rorycallaghan.com/our-3-brains-why-95-of-our-behaviors-are-not-conscious/amp/

Story 2
2. Inge Bretherton, "The Origins of Attachment Theory: John Bowlby and Mary Ainsworth," Stony Brook University Department of Psychology, http://www.psychology.sunysb.edu/attachment/online/inge_origins.pdf

Story 5
3. LaFreniere, L. S., & Newman, M. G. (2019). Exposing worry's deceit: Percentage of untrue worries in generalized anxiety disorder treatment. Behavior Therapy. doi:10.1016/j.beth.2019.07.003

Story 12
4. Tom Sightings, "7 Myths About Millionaires," US News and World Report, November 29, 2018, https://money.usnews.com/money/blogs/on-retirement/articles/7-myths-about-millionaires

Story 14
5. Rakesh Kochhar & Stella Sechopoulos, How the American Middle Class Has Changed in the Past Five Decades," Pew Research Center, April 20, 2022, https://www.pewresearch.org/short-reads/2022/04/20/how-the-american-middle-class-has-changed-in-the-past-five-decades/
6. Joseph E. Stiglitz, "COVID Has Made Global Inequality Much Worse," Scientific American, March 1, 2022, https://www.scientificamerican.com/article/covid-has-made-global-inequality-much-worse/.

Money Made Simple. Elevate Your Life

Follow **@MichaelAnthonyTV**

Instagram

YouTube

The Coolest Cruise Vlog In the World!

Instagram

YouTube

Join the Journey **@SignsSightsSounds**

LEVEL UP YOUR LIFE.

Get the **FREE Workbook** now!

Free Download – Take Action Now!

www.michaelanthonytv.com/**LIFEISDOPE**

LIFE IS DOPE The Official Workbook

BY MICHAEL ANTHONY

SKIP THE HASSLE.

Order your **Professionally Printed Workbook** today!

Scan to Order Here!

www.michaelanthonytv.com/**LIFEISDOPE**

LIFE IS DOPE The Official Workbook
BY MICHAEL ANTHONY

WANT LIFE, MONEY, OR CAREER GUIDANCE?

Get **Exclusive** Coaching & Join a Supportive Community.

Scan to Take the Next Step— Your Dope Life Starts Here!

Past Coaching Clients

"This was the **best decision I made for myself and my business.** Thank you!" - A.J.

"Michael **gave me action steps** to achieve success" - S.D.

"Michael Anthony **is the bomb!**" - C.C

"Michael Anthony is an **expert** in his field" - B.D.

"**Michael has brought confidence in my life and business.** He listens and creates an environment that promotes self development. You feel comfortable showing all your cards, and **you have confidence he'll lead you to make your best plays.** My family is thankful for him." - J.G.

www.michaelanthonytv.com/COACHING

WRITE YOUR OWN STORY
OWN YOUR JOURNEY
CREATE YOUR DOPE LIFE!

Get Your *Journal* Now!

www.michaelanthonytv.com/**LIFEISDOPE**

LIFE IS DOPE by Michael Anthony

SHARE THE LOVE

BUY A COPY FOR A FRIEND!

LIFE IS DOPE

15 STORIES OF HARD-WON HOPE & THE POWER OF PERSEVERANCE

MICHAEL ANTHONY

BULK ORDERS? Visit:

www.michaelanthonytv.com/LIFEISDOPE

LIFE IS DOPE by Michael Anthony